AN ENGLISH GRAMMAR

AN ENGLISH GRAMMAR

THE LANGUAGE BEFORE BABEL

Rudolf Schmid

Waldorf PUBLICATIONS

Waldorf Publications
Research Institute for Waldorf Education
38 Main Street
Chatham, NY 12037

An English Grammar: The Language before Babel by Rudolf Schmid
Editor: David S. Mitchell
Typing: Betsy Petering
Proofreading: Nicole Fields

ISBN: 978-1-888365-15-3

CURRICULUM SERIES

The Publications Committee of the Research Institute is pleased to bring forward this publication as part of its Curriculum Series. The thoughts and ideas represented herein are solely those of the author and do not necessarily represent any implied criteria set by Waldorf Publications. It is our intention to stimulate as much writing and thinking as possible about our curriculum, including diverse views. Please contact us at patrice@waldorf-research.org with feedback on this publication as well as requests for future work.

CONTENTS

PREFACE

THE ENGLISH LANGUAGE, complex as it is, can be seen in a single form as we see the individual figure of a man. To perceive this form we must start from a definite point of view, namely, from the doctrine of the sentence. Sentence comes from the Latin "*sententia*" which means to feel or to sense. This sensing or feeling refers to the inner life of man, not to his bodily form. It means, simply, the forward moving of the human soul or self. This soul movement comes to expression as speaking and is called "language" from the Latin lingua: the tongue. Speech is human, not animal nor angelic. Only the human tongue can form the air into the sounds of real words that carry the meanings of thought and link man's life to the life of the world. This linking of human life to the Universal Life forms the basis of all speaking whose foundation and communicating vessel is the Sentence. The Sentence is the living form of language, just as the physical body gives the outer form to man. Grammar, from the Greek "Gramma," signifying that language grasped in the concrete: the skeleton within it. Grammatically speaking there are six ways to view the Sentence. It is the determination of these six ways of viewing the Sentence which are to constitute the contents of this book.

INTRODUCTION

This is no ordinary run-of-the-mill Grammar book. Of such there are surely enough in print already, good and bad. This book is rather of a different sort. It has a quite different purport and has been written to serve a different but distinct purpose. Herein the attempt is made to grasp English Grammar in a single living whole, as the mind cognizes in what the human eye grasps as the outer form of an object, and the idea indwelling it, and through such a comprehending grasp to gaze deeper into the true nature of language, as such, and into the nature of the being who speaks, namely Man.

What is normally set down as a bundle of rules and forms of usage, without any essential order and interconnection, classified in the traditional way of mixing in motley manner the proper levels of conception, often appearing intellectually dry and abstract, hence more a burden than a balm to the mind, is seen with this book, which perceives these grammatical elements in a pro-portion transparent to their truth, to be the interrelating, interdependent members of a real entity known to us by the name Logos or the Creative Word.

Out of dead, intellectualized, traditionally bound grammar rules, the lines of a definite life, a real form becomes clear. This is man's own greater dimension, a higher level of his being. To this being, freed from the state and slavery of these traditionally fixed grammatical forms and born into more exact scientifically seen lines, this book is a guide. It is a guide to that being man, in that he speaks, reveals, yet unbeknown to himself. When he begins to grasp the "Self," he forever is speaking, begins to grasp it from out of his own mouth, so to speak, then indeed, will its reality validate and become of real value to him. Man shall come to know himself, who he truly is, and from being the mere soul machine he is today, still dedicated to the "rockets red glare and bombs bursting in air," he will ascend in the dignity of his own person to become a self-moving spiritual force.

The lead-lines herein brought to relief are the first drawn features of this Human Logos Life at the heart of all speaking and writing. In contemplating them the reader is led to an inner certainty of knowledge respecting the language as a totality; and simultaneously is encouraged to partake of its creative life and develop a definite individual style through active participation in the exercises outlined herein. This book should therefore serve as a "standard text" for teachers, who, so oriented in the language, can better compass the vast seas of instruction, or for those versed in the language to a degree needed to rouse their zeal to this venture.

Originally arising as a need for a proper text in teaching English to Germans, it is by no means limited in its signifying import, but meaningful as a structure for every language in its turn. The features herein "English perceived" can be seen in every human tongue, just as the human face, though individually varied according to country and climate, is in its essential composition universal. Every language, however, brings some particular feature of the General Logos Life into characteristic relief, as does English the Continuous Verb Form with the consequent use of the present participle, or German the peculiar use of the Dative Case, ·and the word order of the verb that follows thereupon. It would be possible in the light ofthE foundational conception herein put forth, to bring the Grammar of all"other languages into a true perspective, explicate proportionally the latent form therein, and enliven in them the sense for the Word as it works individually qualifying in each particular tongue.

To master the Grammar of Language in the form herein presented, is to bring clarity into otherwise misty regions of consciousness, straighten the otherwise bent lines of mental life, setting these into erect posture, and to introduce a certain hygiene into man's inner life, where an otherwise unkempt ignorance holds sway. In this century language is already beginning to decay and disintegrate in the mouths of men and women everywhere. Speaking, as well as writing, undergoes the death of being over-simplified, vulgarized, and atomized. A thousand diseases the language suffers. Before this process of decay overreaches the bounds of a natural sanity, it were well, we believe, to make the effort to counter it. With this book we have sought to give the soil wherein the seed of such an effort may be profitably planted.

Rachel Carson has told us how the birds are dying. How, being increasingly poisoned, they no longer appear at their favorite places in the trees, by the river bank, on the meadows, are no longer seen or heard where once they were wont to fill the air with colored radiance and cheerful sound. So we must sadly perceive that language in its colorful, finely formed, multitudinous, rich, and nobly fashioned being is dying in the throats and on the lips of men, that the winged life of the word is dying out through the suffocating poison of intellectuality and common vulgarity, and the dry utilitarian superficiality of its use and comprehension.

This trend must cease. We must resurrect the language in our use and comprehension of it, rescue it from this dying and decay. It lives, a being in its own right, as well as being the means for communication of thought and ought, as such, to be grasped. Man's speaking (and writing) should become penetrated through and through with the light of his own consciousness, that this mere vessel of thought be irradiated with self-knowledge and impulse to creative life, and that out of it again flow forth those flights of winged words, whose sounds cheer men to new hope, and appeal to the noblest of their intents.

What a noble being is a man when the spirit of the word dwells in his heart, and flows from his lips, or though his pen, in harmony with that deeper sense for beauty all men cherish, and, no matter how mummified by the plasters of civilization, nevertheless, still possess! It is to this sense also, that such a book as this appeals. Were the awakened sense of speech herein striven toward to be realized in him, then could man's whole nature be rejuvenated.

But allons! Reader. Yours is now the task. Do but work it through in solitude or the society of students, tutor, or friends—for it is a "handbook" to be worked, as much as it provides entertainment in simply reading—and it shall animate your whole regard for the English Tongue, deepen, it is hoped, your insight into language as such, and enkindle the flame of a true inspiration in your heart. For it is the heart, Reader, the language of the heart that with all our speaking we at the last desire to wake.

—Rudolf Schmid

Chapter I
SENTENCE STRUCTURE

The first way to see a sentence is in the perspective of its structure. And this in its prime elements is:

Subject   Predicate

Predicate comes from the Latin "*predicare*," to proclaim. So we have the subject and its proclamation, what is proclaimed forth from it, like the trumpet proclaiming the word of the king. This predicating by the subject is always done through the verb, from the Latin "*verbum*," meaning, simply, "word," so that to simplify terms, we may call the predicate: verb. No sentence is without subject and verb. For it to be a sentence it must have both. The simplest sentence is:

Upon this structure all sentences, no matter how complicated, are built. Distinguish subject and verb in the following:

The rose is red.

Deep blue is the sky.

With flitting swing the swallow darts under the red barn roof.

Who is coming for dinner?

Because of the rain we called off the open air concert and played indoors instead.

Every subject has the possibility of being apposed, i.e. of taking an Apposition, and every verb explicitly or implicitly points its action towards an Object, so that the complete structure of a full sentence is:

7

APPOSITION

An Apposition is a phrase equivalent to a noun and placed, for the most part, directly after it, as an ambassador, bearing the seal and significance of the king, represents "appositively" the kingdom. It therefore modifies both subject and object(s) and can appear as well in the predicate, i.e. after the verb, as next to the subject.

Abraham Lincoln, the sixteenth President of the United States, was born in a log cabin.

Hamlet, Shakespeare's most famous play, was written in 1601.

After walking hours on winding paths through the dark woods, they finally came to their destination: a little house nestled in a sunlit clearing like a diamond lying on the jeweler's velvet.

At Dodona, one of the less frequented oracles, in the ancient days of Greece, the priestesses read the thoughts of the God, Zeus, in the rustling leaves of the Oak, a very special and sacred tree to the ancient Greek people.

"In the year 1799, Captain Amasa Delano, of Duxbury in Massachusetts, commanding a large sealer and general trader, lay at anchor with a valuable cargo, in the harbor of Santa Maria—a small, desert, uninhabited island toward the southern extremity of the long coast of Chile."

—Herman Melville, *Benito Cereno*

Appositions add color to writing. Make a series of sentences apposing both subject and object. Appose the following nouns in sentences: river, mountain, sun, woman, New York.

OBJECT

There are three kinds of object:

1) *Direct Object*
2) *Indirect Object*
3) *Prepositional Object*

1) A *Direct Object* is the noun placed directly after the verb which receives into itself the full action of the verb.

Brutus stabbed Caesar.

I love you.

In the winter deep he slept a long sleep.

"So God created man in his own image, in the image of God created he him, male and female created he them."

—Moses

2) An *Indirect Object* is a second object which receives the verb action as already objectified in the Direct Object. It comes to use only with certain verbs whose action carries the implicit reference to a receiver and it has the character of a Prepositional Phrase.

Raleigh gave roses to the queen.

Ask me no questions and I'll tell you no lies.

What did Stanley say to Livingstone upon finding him in the interior of Africa?

3) A *Prepositional Object* is a noun following a preposition together with which it constitutes the "prepositional phrase," the most common unit in all language.

Up, up into the blue the broad-winged eagle flew.

"Once upon a midnight dreary, while I pondered, weak and weary, over many a quaint and curious volume of forgotten lore."

—Edgar Allen Poe, "The Raven"

"Shall I compare thee to a summers day..."

—Shakespeare

Read what's writ between the lines.

A noun may also follow an adjective or a verbal (Infinitive or Gerund) as in the following sentences:

He's worth his weight in gold.

"O my Love's like a red red rose."

—Robert Burns

Eating pumpkin pie is a Thanksgiving custom in America.

For what does the heart yearn more than to go home!

Yet, though often termed "object of the adjective" or "object of the verbal," not standing in any relation to the flow of the verb action, neither directly, indirectly, or prepositionally, these nouns actually fit into another aspect of Grammar.

Form sentences employing the three types of objects in various and interesting ways.

Predicate nominatives (nouns) and predicate adjectives are often thought to be a part of the Sentence Structure. A predicate noun following the verb "to be" in sentences such as:

The earth is a star.

Man is a being who speaks, thinks, and walks erect.

corresponds to the direct object following a transitive verb. But all being (all forms of "to be") is a state or condition not an action, so that the noun following the verb "to be" is in equivalence not in apposition to the subject, is the subject, in whole or part, repeated. The noun that is the object of the true verb action is like a wheat kernel used to make bread, and then eaten: whereas the noun following the verb condition "to be" is the same kernel used to plant and grow more wheat. Thus the structure of a sentence remains in essence.

Analyze the composition of the following sentences in terms of the four elements of their structure, keeping in mind that some are "complex" sentences containing dependent clauses with subjects and verbs of their own.

"The name Ivanhoe was no sooner pronounced than it flew from mouth to mouth with all the celerity with which eagerness could convey and curiosity receive it."

—Sir Walter Scot, *Ivanhoe*

"Upon my return to the United States a few months ago, after the extraordinary series of adventures in the South Seas and elsewhere, of which an account is given in the following pages, accident threw me into the society of several gentlemen in Richmond, Virginia, who felt deep interest in all matters relating to the regions I had visited, and who were constantly urging it upon me, as a duty, to give my narrative to the public."

—Edgar Allen Poe, *Narrative of A. Gordon Pym*

"At this precise moment, however, the Cointet Brothers, paper manufacturers, purchased the second printers license in Angouleme."

—Balzac, *Lost Illusions*

"Upon gaining a less remote view, the ship, when made singly visible on the verge of the leaden-hued swells, with the shreds of fog here and there raggedly furring her, appeared like a white washed monastery after a thunderstorm, seen perched upon some dun cliff among the Pyrenees."

—Herman Melville, *Benito Cereno*

Chapter II
SENTENCE COMPOSITION OR PARTS OF SENTENCE

The second way of viewing a sentence is to see the parts or component units out of which it is composed. They are three:

    1) Words

    2) Phrases

    3) Clauses

All sentences are composed of words, but some words combine into groups having a characteristic attribute and use, and are called a phrase or clause. Sentences of mere words are:

    It was high noon and the sun was shining brightly.

    "Roll on, thou deep and dark blue ocean, roll."

             —Byron

    "O Death where is thy sting? O grave where is thy victory?"

             —St. Paul

PHRASES

Of Phrases there are three basic kinds:

    1) Prepositional Phrase

    2) Infinitive Phrases

    3) Participial Phrases

        Past   Present
    Participial Participial

Prepositional Phrases

The prepositional phrase places the verb action in a context of time and space, qualifies it in life and the world, renders it concrete.

Over mountains, down valleys, through forests and fields, cross rivers and plains, on foot with their shields and spears in their hands, from their lips the cry pealing in thunderous tones to the people upgaining against their onslaught the Barbarians marched south toward the sea.

"The Bells of Youth are ringing in the gateways of the south: The bannerettes of green are not unfurled; spring has risen with a laugh, a wild-rose in her mouth. And is singing, singing, singing, thro' the world."

—F McCloud, *The Bells of Youth*

Count the prepositional phrases in the following sentence:

They battled on the slope of a hill by a flowing river near the castle under a hot sun at midday; in clashing armor with flashing broad swords, as was the style in those days, they fought for hour on hour, till even, in the red glow of the setting sun, mixed in melancholy with the blood flown from their wounds glistening like scarlet dew upon that gallant field.

You should find eighteen. The core of this sentence is "they battled, they fought." Render the following sentence cores to a full picture by adding prepositional phrases before and after.

We walked

The house stands

The eagle flies

She ate

He telephoned

The lovers kissed

I read

The ship sailed

Remember the prepositional phrase can be used both as adjective modifying the nouns (subject and object) or as adverb modifying the verb.

Using the following prepositions: in, beside, along, on, by, out of, away, up, into, round, at, to, of, out, across, down to, over, upon, into, through, between, next to, above, against, fill in the blanks below:

A: _____ the river stood a hut. _____ the roof was a chimney _____ which rose smoke _____ the evening sky. The travelers knocked _____ the door _____ the hut. They wanted a ride _____ the river. The ferryman came _____ of the hut and led them _____ the water's edge. They got _____ the boat and he shoved _____ into the stream. The red glow of the sun shone _____ the water as it lapped _____ the sides of the boat cutting _____ the low waves. No word passed _____ them. The silence was only broken _____ the hooting _____ an owl. Deep _____ the forest the call of the cuckoo floated _____ the evening air. The strangers sat _____ each other engrossed _____ thought. The stars _____ them sparkled. It took a half hour to get _____ the river. Gently the boat rubbed _____ the bank. Once _____ the other side, the strangers disembarked, took _____ their purse and gave the fare _____ the ferryman. He nodded _____ them, turned _____, and rowed _____. They walked side _____ side _____ the river bank, talking together _____ the rising light of the moon.

Using the following prepositions: ahead of, with, due to, in spite of, toward, because of, on, unto, after, past, according to, apart from, without, instead of, in place of, as a result of, since, except, contrary to, by virtue of, for, in view of, via, onto, before, by means of, up to, fill in the blanks below.

B: He walked _____ the hill, his horse _____ him. All day he had ridden _____ eating and drinking. _____ this lack of sustenance, he was not over weary, but just _____ his hunger he was anxious to make ground _____ sundown. The long valley lay _____ him, but hurrying he rode _____ even pace, _____ his horse's exhaustion.

He rode _____ sage brush and cactus, and _____ an occasional coyote met no one _____, of course, the rattle snakes. He had been riding thus _____ three o'clock, when, _____ tripping over a large stone, his horse threw him _____ the dusty desert floor. _____ giving his body a graceful twist he landed unhurt. _____ a while he continued _____ foot. _____ the long distance yet to cover, he couldn't expect to arrive _____ nightfall. So, _____ cowboy custom he unpacked his gear and lit a fire. _____ his expectations he had enough grub for a meal. _____ his superior marksmanship he managed to slay a rabbit which had jumped _____ the fire, attracted by its flickering. _____ dry bread he now had fresh meat. He gave thanks _____ God, and _____ eating heartily, resting his head _____ his saddle he fell asleep.

INFINITIVE

Infinitives or infinitive phrases are bountiful and make speech poignant. They refer to a verb action in its unconditioned "idea-form" before it is set through the prepositional phrase into time and space and rendered concrete.

All ideas, so far as they are purposes in human will or forces in nature, are first infinitive in form and then only prepositional in their realization; like arrows in the quiver yet unstrung, unnamed, unshod.

"To err is human, to forgive is divine."
　　—Pope

"Yesterday afternoon set in misty and cold. I had half a mind to spend it by my study fire, instead of wading through heath and mud to Wuthering Heights."
　　—Emily Bronte

"But the quality of the imagination is to flow, and not to freeze."
　　—Ralph Waldo Emerson

When, in the course of human events, it becomes necessary for one people to dissolve the political bands which have connected them with another, and to assume among the powers of the earth the separate and equal station to which the laws of nature and of nature's God entitle them, a decent respect to the opinions of mankind requires that they should declare the causes which impel them to the separation."

—Thomas Jefferson

An extraordinary and most famous example of the infinitive phrase is given by Hamlet:

"To be, or not to be: that is the question; Whether 'tis nobler in the mind to suffer
The slings and arrows of outrageous fortune, Or to take arms against a sea of troubles, And
by opposing end them? To die; to sleep; No more; and by a sleep to say we end
The heart-ache and the thousand natural shocks That flesh is heir to, 'tis a consummation
Devoutly to be wish'd ... "

—Shakespeare

Analyze all the previous sentence-texts to tell how the infinitives or infinitive phrases are used therein, and write a series of sentences employing them as subjects, appositive, object, adverb, etc.

PARTICIPIAL

The participial phrase, both present and past, is a common and colorful element of modification. They are by nature adjectival and either flow like summer streams or contract into pregnant form like the winter earth.

Suffusing sweet perfume and sporting rich red tones, the roses, wreathing o'er the trellis, gave a gladness to the scene.

Girded with lion skins, tanned in tropic suns and toughened by the tests of time—thus did Hercules approach Prometheus on the rock.

The present participle is formed by adding "ing" to the infinitive: being, singing, swimming, hearing, etc. The past participle of regular verbs is formed, as the past tense, by adding "ed": slashed, drenched, bedraggled, propped, etc.

The participial phrases are formed in principle by detaching the participles from their context in the verb and placing them before the subject as adjective. What is first an action becomes an attribute:

The girl was singing…

Singing, the girl… —Present

The apples had ripened…

Having ripened the apples… —Past

The movement is like jumping rope. What was verb action performed by the subject (in front) becomes the adjectival attribute or property of the subject itself (behind). The subject, thus modified, is freed for new verb action. Once formed the participial phrases can be placed for modification anywhere in the sentence.

She lay in bed propped up on giant pillows.

Johnny, soaked to the skin, came running up the porch stairs.

Unimpressed by the splendors of the court, the philosopher turned to the contemplation of eternal things.

Howling wildly the wolves neared the fire.

The stranger, tossing custom to the winds, embraced him heartily. They entered the room on tip toe, not daring to breathe.

A good example of the space and freedom created through the use of the participial is this passage from Whitman's "Song of Open Road":

"From this hour I ordain myself loos'd of limits and imaginary lines, Going where I list, my own master total and absolute,
Listening to others, considering well what they say,
Pausing, searching, receiving, contemplating,
Gently, but with undeniable will, divesting myself of the holds that would hold me."

Summing up the three types of phrases in the following sentence:

"Upon a white horse, poised gracefully in the saddle, singing sweet lays, and happy to be alive, he came riding up to join us in the chase."

Distinguish them from one another. The sentence core is "he came," the rest is modification. So we see how to paint with the phrases of the language.

Now detach the participles out of the following (groups of) sentences and place them in the sentence as modifiers of the subject, dropping unnecessary words and substituting noun as subject for pronoun when necessary. Example:

The valley was shrouded in rose hue. It lay hidden in the hills. Shrouded in rose hue, the valley lay hidden in the hills.

For Past Participle Phrases

He bathed himself in the milk of the stream, anointed himself with the oils of the East, swathed himself in skins of the leopard, crowned himself with the laurel leaf and strode forth to meet the queen.

The ship had been battered by inexorable waves, and blown by ceaseless winds, and blistered by the unrelenting downpour of solar heat, before it finally entered the harbor.

The herd was rounded up and guided into the corral. There it awaited slaughter.

She sent him the ring. It was wrapped in silk. It was scented in perfume. It was engraved with the fondest name.

He was schooled in thought. He had been armed through the discipline of his order. The Dominican monk launched his attack against the Arabs.

Our food has been sprayed with mineral dust. It has been harvested unripe. It has been frozen solid or dried out for preservation. It has, that is, been literally deprived of almost all its essential nourishing value. And thus, as mere bulk, it is set before us at table.

For Present Participle Phrases

The day is dawning in dim light. It breaks.

The clouds are drifting across the sky. They lace and cushion the blue.

The boy was smiling form cheek to cheek. He was holding a basket full of ripe red berries. He ran home from the strawberry patch.

The poet sat writing in the twilight. He was dreaming of days to come.

She was baking pie and canning peaches; she was cleaning (the) house and weeding the garden; she was writing letters and doing handicrafts with the children; she was darning socks and styling clothes. And so she spent the days.

The horses could be seen a mile away. They were racing over the plain and were kicking up a cloud of prairie dust.

The moon is shining over the tranquil lake. It creates a silver ripple upon its mirror-like surface. It is shedding its magic through the darkened night air.

Now write a series of sentences with participial phrases, using among other verbs, the following: to gray, to battle, to adorn, to arm, to substantiate, to honor, to revere, to wed, to pave, to batter, to blow, to bless, to chuck, to throw, to flush, to furrow, to strip, to boast, to soften, to harden, to warm, to entertain. Be aware of whether the past participle is put in the active or passive voice. In the former case the auxiliary verb "to have" is employed.

Active   Having weathered the calms and storms of the voyage the vessel sailed safely into the harbor.

Passive   Driven and drenched by rough rains the plane rolled onto the runway.

The Gerund is a present participle used as noun, e.g. Swimming is a great sport. Out of the Gerund a phrasal unit can be constructed:

Your learning English is simply a matter of practice and will power.

I was amazed at her being selected for the part.

In this Grammar we shall classify the use of the Gerund under "*Participial Phrase.*"

Combine the three types of phrases variously together in many sentences, illustrating their essential, creative, and supplemental character in the composition of a sentence.

CLAUSES

In all of language there are but three kinds of clauses:

1) Subordinate Clause

2) Relative Clause

3) Noun Clause

Although all clauses are "subordinate" being dependent upon the main clause or independent sentence, we reserve this name for a clause introduced by a subordinate conjunction. A list of such is given in the next chapter. An example of subordination through a subordinate conjunction is:

The Nile floods its banks each year when the sun rises in the star of Sirius.

The major sentence is:

The Nile floods its banks each year;

its minor clause is:

when the sun rises in the star of Sirius.

Both have subjects and verbs, and the distinction the clause upholds over against the phrase is that it possesses a subject and a verb, whereas the latter does not. Other examples:

"Here, under leave of Brutus and the rest, for Brutus is an honorable man; so are they all, all honorable men; come I to speak in Caesar's funeral."
—Shakespeare, *Julius Caesar*

"Fortune is like a market; where many times, if you can stay a little, the price will fall."
—Lord Bacon

"Just above yon sandy bar,
As the day grows fainter and dimmer,
Lonely and lovely, a single star
Lights the air with a dusky glimmer."
—Henry Wadsworth Longfellow

"With her native energy of character, and rare capacity, it could not entirely cast her off, although it had set a work upon her, more intolerable to a woman's heart than that which branded the brow of Cain."
—Nathaniel Hawthorne, *The Scarlet Letter*

SUBORDINATE CLAUSE

The **Subordinate Clause** is always adverbial and acts as a qualification to the verb action. Every existent verb action whether explicitly qualified by subordinate clauses or not, is carried out in an aura of such qualification, as sunlight acting through moist air always produces a rainbow, whether or not the rainbow appears visibly to the eye.

For example, if one says, "I speak poetry out loud," there is always a because, a before and after, a while, an unless, an although, a where, when, so (that), until, if, and in order that, and since, and as, and the several other subordinating conjunctions implicitly present founding the action. One or two may be expressed because pertinent and relevant to the situation in which the action is executed: e.g. I speak poetry out loud a) because it is a good training for the ear, and, of course; b) in order to form the voice; c) after dinner Sunday evenings ; d) when I am inspired; e) although my landlady sometimes complains, etc. The rest are latent and make up the unspoken background of the action. As an exercise, choose a particular action (verb in context) and clothe it with all the qualifying subordinate clauses, if possible, in order to create a sense for the mood and quality of each conjunctive qualification. Do this with various verbs until you acquire flexibility in dealing with the whole scale of subordination.

Use the proper subordinate conjunction in subordinating the following pairs of sentences. Make sure the main sentence contains the main idea, the subordinate, the subordinate idea.

He loved to walk The trees were full of the song of birds.

The werewolves roam at night. The moon is full.

The sun was shining. It was raining.

The roses bloomed and bloomed. Every bud had flowered.

The sun began rising in the sign of Pisces. Mankind has developed from the closed consciousness of the middle ages to the cosmopolitanism of the 20th century.

An Englishman stands. There is England.

Nerofiddled. Romeburned.

There shall be suffering in the world. There is evil in the world.

He came walking up the lane. She saw him and ran out of the house to meet him.

The rain has ceased to fall and the sun shines through the clouds. A rainbow arcs across the sky.

The lightning strikes. There is an uncanny stillness in the air.

The summer days are all so full of sunny warmth. All the wheat field will be a golden sea.

Then we can see the sunrise. We shall set forth early in the morn. Man can speak. He has been built to speak.

The odds are against us. We shall attempt it again and again. They were Indians. They ran around barefoot.

She managed to fight her way to the newstand. The crowd in the station was enormous.

We have been made in the thought of God. Thinking, we may become a God.

The angels rejoice. A sinner is converted on earth

The leaves will not change till October. The frost comes on St. Michael's day.

RELATIVE CLAUSE

The second kind of clause is the **Relative Clause**.

The cat which crossed his path was black.

That group of stars that you see in the sky is the constellation of Orion.

Of the famous women in history one who has been most unjustly defamed is Mary Stuart of Scotland.

The Relative Clause is always an adjective which modifies a noun: "which" for impersonal objects (things), "who" (whom, whose) for persons, and "that" for either things or persons. There being no regular manifestation of "cases" in English apart from the personal pronouns, these words remain constant. Only "who" changes to "whom" when in the objective (dative and accusative) case with or without prepositions and to "whose" when the possessive (genitive) is meant. The relative clause enables us to predicate additionally of a noun without writing another sentence.

"The Supreme Critic on the errors of the past and the present, and the only prophet of that which must be, is that great nature in which we rest as the earth lies in the soft arms of the atmosphere; that Unity, that Over-Soul within which every man's particular being is contained and made one with all other; that common heart of which all sincere converasation is the worship, to which all right action is submission; that overpowering reality which confutes our tricks and talents, and constrains everyone to pass for what he is, and to speak from his character and not from his tongue, and which evermore tends to pass into our thought and hand and become wisdom and virtue and power and beauty."

—Ralph Waldo Emerson, "The Over-Soul"

Render one of the sentences in the following pairs relative to the other, the less important or the more important.

The tree stood in the middle of the forest. It was the mightiest of all.

New York City was built on the island of Manhattan. The island of Manhattan was bought from the Indians for 29 dollars.

The Mona Lisa is a painting of a woman. It was painted by Leonardo. The say she is smiling because she knows she has conceived a child.

A woman named Bettina arranged a meeting between Goethe and Beethoven in Weimar. She was a friend of Goethe. She had visited Beethoven out of admiration for the man and his works.

The first actor in history was Thespis. He may be said to have started Greek Drama by introducing a player in addition to the chorus.

"Ea" is a vowel combination in the English language. It is of all of them the most unusually pronounced.

Ideas are often expressed in pictures. These are rich and can be easily remembered. We will make a point of writing sentences for exercise. This, I believe, shall be helpful.

Write fifteen sentences in which relative clauses are used to modify the nouns (subject, apposition, object). Write sentences with relative clauses modifying the following nouns: horse, mountain, valley, play, personality, constellation, historical epoch, goal, virtues.

NOUN CLAUSES

The third kind of clause in language is the **Noun Clause**. It is so named because it provides a substitute for a noun (or pronoun), hence it replaces subject or object.

Taking the sentence:

That is still a moot point among whalemen.

we substitute a noun clause for the subject "that."

Whether or not the spout of a whale is pure air or a mixture of air and water is still a moot point among whalemen.

Or for the object "something" in the sentence:

He knew something.

we substitute the clause:

He knew how one could get to the essence of things.

Other examples:

They walked through what seemed to be an unending passageway.

"We hold these truths to be self evident: that all men are created equal; that they are endowed by their Creator with certain inherent and inalienable rights; that among these are life, liberty, and the pursuit of happiness; that to secure these rights, governments are instituted among men, deriving their just powers from the consent of the governed; that whenever any form of government becomes destructive to these ends, it is the right of the people to alter or to abolish it, and to institute new government, laying its foundation on such principles, and organizing its powers in such form, as to them shall seem most likely to effect their safety and happiness."

—Thomas Jefferson, *The Declaration of Independence*

We couldn't figure out what it was, where it came from, when and how it had got there, who had discovered it, and why in God's name it had ever entered our midst.

A Noun Clause, as either subject or object, does an interesting service in the language. It takes the simple, linguistic, fact expressing world life, stated or asked, e.g.:

Easter is on the first Sunday after the first full moon after the Vernal Equinox.

A storm is coming up.

How do you get to Tipperary?

Where do the wild geese spend the winter?

and transforming into property (attribute), re-embodies it as a fact of the subject's inner life:

Everyone knows from school that Easter is on the first Sunday after the first full moon

after the Vernal Equinox

The old mare feels in her bones that a storm is coming up.

The Irishman knows how you get to Tipperary.

The children often wonder where the wild geese spend the winter.

The whole sentential content of consciousness is thus lifted into the inner life. Hence, noun clauses can follow all verbs expressing human soul life: to believe, to feel, to know, to understand, to trust, to doubt, to suspect, to suppose, to hope, to wish, et. al. The further consequence of this service of the Noun Clause is that it is the vehicle man has at his disposal in speech to reiterate his fellow human being's statements and thoughts: in Indirect Speech we use the Noun Clause:

Direct *Speech*	"I will arise and go now, and go to Innisfree, And a small cabin build there, of clay and wattles made." 　　　　　　　—Yeats, "The Lake Isle of Innisfree"
Indirect *Speech* (Present)	He says that he will arise and go now, and go to Innisfree, Speech and a small cabin build there of clay and wattles made.
(Past)	He said that he would arise and go now, and go to Innisfree, and a small cabin build there of clay and wattles made.

Thus through the Noun Clause is re-given the facts of the world and the speech of fellowmen. As exercise put the following into Indirect Speech:

"Hello," he shouted, and asked: "Are you going to the wedding?"

"Is there a wedding?" I answered, "And who would be marrying in this weather?" I added musingly.

"There's an old proverb that says: 'He who marries in foul weather has a fair way.'" was his further reply.

"'Tis wonderful, the ways of the Lord," I retorted, "but what of those then who marry in fair weather? Does the opposite hold true?"

"Not so," said he, "but the proverb reads on: 'The fair-weather bride bears sun-hearted children.'"

Put the following into Direct Speech:

He often thought how curious it was that the ocean waves roll in opposite directions. He asked himself whether the winds were ever completely still. He knew that the earth revolves around the sun, but saw that the sun revolves around the earth. He assured himself that were his thinking and perceiving in harmony he would know the whole truth. And he divined that when he should learn it, he could certainly toss his head and shoulders in a more carefree manner.

As a further exercise put the following text, which is in the form of Direct Speech, into the Indirect Speech form:

John informed us: "He came to see them, brought many fine things; some they have used, others they have put on display, and still others, left, as it were, unused on the shelf." He told us: "He showed them the way to make proper use of the things he had brought, the way to care for them and keep them in repair."

"What a wealth of goods they now have," he exclaimed, amazed, "but do they know how to promote them among their fellows?"

"This would be a great benefit to those involved and to the community at large," he mused, and ended with the expressed hope: "May a fresh wind fill their sails!"

Complete the following sentences by filling out the noun clauses:

Whether or not … … … was a mystery to them.

The belief that … … … is common among the natives.

Louis's guests were whomever … … … .

Who can really tell why … … … .

Scotland Yard is certain of what … … … .

Buffalo graze where … … … .

When … … … determines the rising and ebbing of the tides.

Look to see whose … … … .

Who … … … became clear to use all with time.

Nouns, from the Latin *"Nomen"* meaning name, are the names of things and are attained in thinking as answer to the questions we pose to life and the world, through the words: what, why, where, when, how, who (whom, whose), whether, whatever, wherever, whenever, whoever, and the unnamed "that." Hence Noun Clauses, which serve as explication or description of the noun, begin with these words.

Write examples of 15 noun clauses using them as both subjects and objects (all three types).

Reviewing the clauses and their uses we have:

Subordinate Clause	—	Adverb
Relative Clause	—	Adjective
Noun Clause	—	Noun

Metaphorically speaking the **Subordinate Clause**, adverbially modifying the verb action from all sides, is as an eagle constantly on the wing, or as the feathers of that wing arrayed in a head dress round the head, just as the subordinate qualifications surround, whether expressed or not, qua conditioning thoug.hts, the idea of each verb action.

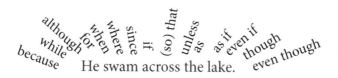

The **Relative Clause** is like the lion springing forward in a rhythmic sort of way adjectivally out of the noun: a forward progressing continuum which is maintained creatively by ever new discrete units breathed forth fresh from the subject:

That being who gardened in Eden, who housed through the island of Atlantis, who survived the great flood, who worshipped Brahma in old India, who sang the Avestas with Zoroaster in Persia, who performed the "sacred wedding" atop the Ziggurat in Sumer, who searched the secrets of time and eternity in the pyramids of Egypt, who wandered from Ur in Chaldea to the Holy Land, who sought the Golden Fleece and listened to the oracles in ancient Greece, who witnessed the Event of Golgatha, who built the splendors of Byzantium and the Santa Sophia, who lived through the European Dark Ages, who battled for Christ in the Crusades, who folded his hands in prayer under the arches of the

Gothic Cathedral, who woke to Nature and the Earth and discovered the World Ocean in the Renaissance, who has succeeded the strife of Churches and State, founded the Age of Intellectual Enlightenment, established Modern Science, and who entered the 20th century through two World Wars with a will to experience the Higher Worlds—that being is Man!

As a grazing beast of pasture, buffalo or cow, heavily bound to the earth, the Noun Clause, always a bit clumsy, rests in its subject or object-place in the sentence.

Parsifal saw that Amfortas was wounded, but neglected to ask what had caused the wound. Learn to recognize clauses by analyzing the following texts for all types, at the same time noting all phrases. Then practice reading them aloud until the music and movement of modification in the language become familiar.

"During the whole of a dull, dark, and soundless day in the autumn of the year, when the clouds hung oppressively low in the heavens, I had been passing alone, on horseback, through a singularly dreary tract of country, and at length found myself, as the shades of the evening drew on, within view of the melancholy House of Usher."
—Edgar Allen Poe

"A sky-hawk that tauntingly had followed the main-truck downwards from its natural home among the stars, pecking at the flag, and incommoding Tashtego there; this bird now chanced to intercept its broad fluttering wing between the hammer and the wood; and simultaneously feeling that ethereal thrill, the submerged savage beneath, in his death-gasp, kept his hammer frozen there; and so the bird of heaven, with archangelic shrieks, and his imperial beak thrust upwards, and his whole captive form folded in the flag of Ahab, went down with his ship, which, like Satan, would not sink to hell till she had dragged a living part of heaven along with her, and helmeted herself with it."
—Herman Melville, *Moby Dick*

"But it is time to tell the truth; though it requires some courage to avow it in an age and country, in which disquisitions on all subjects, not privileged to adopt technical terms or scientific symbols, must be addressed to the public."
—S.T. Coleridge

What course mankind as a whole will take in the 20th century, which shall be determined by the choice of every single individual man or woman, since "mankind" is composed of the individual men and women, living or dead, shall, by the events taking place within the next decade, be once and for all proclaimed.

"When at last they had worked round into the Pacific her spars and sails were so damaged, and so inadequately handled by the surviving mariners, most of whom were become invalids, that unable to lay her northerly course by the wind, which was powerful, the unmanageable ship, for successive days and nights, was blown north westward, where the breeze suddenly deserted her, in unknown waters, to sultry calms."
—Herman Melville, *Benito Cereno*

"Nevertheless he submitted to be kissed willingly enough, though Maggie hung on his neck in rather strangling fashion, while his blue-gray eyes wandered towards the croft and the lambs and the river, where he promised himself that he would begin to fish the first thing tomorrow morning."

—George Eliot, *The Mill on the Floss*

"Whatever was the original reason of its adoption, which is unknown, I am only putting on it its popular, its recognized sense, when I say that a University should teach universal knowledge."

—Cardinal Newman

"There is grandeur in this view of life, with its several powers, having been originally breathed by the Creator into a few forms or into one; and that whilst the planet has gone cycling on according to the fixed law of gravity, from so simple a beginning endless forms most beautiful and most wonderful have been, and are being, evolved."

—Charles Darwin, *The Origin of Species*

"But father had been used to think, that any man, who was comfortable inside his own coat and waistcoat, deserved to have no other set, unless he would strike a blow for them."

—R. D. Blackmore, *Lorna Doone*

"That nameless and infinitely delicate aroma of inexpressible tenderness and attentiveness which, in every refined and honorable attachment, is contemporary with the courtship, and precedes the final bans and rite; but which, like the bouquet of the costliest German wines, too often evaporates upon pouring love out to drink, in the disenchanting glasses of the matrimonial days and nights; this highest and airiest thing in the whole compass of the experience of our mortal life; this heavenly evanescence—still further etherealised in the filial breast—was for Mary Glendinning, now not very far from her grand climacteric, miraculously revived in the courteous lover-like adoration of Pierre."

—Herman Melville, *Pierre*

"Wherever snow falls or water flows or birds fly, wherever day and night meet in twilight, wherever the blue heaven is hung by clouds or sown with stars, wherever are forms with transparent boundaries, wherever are outlets into celestial space, wherever is danger, and awe, and love—there is Beauty, plenteous as rain, shed for thee, and though thou shouldst walk the world over, thou shalt not be able to find a condition inopportune or ignoble."

—Ralph Waldo Emerson, "The Poet"

"Come, said my Soul
Such verses for my Body let us write, (for we are one)
That should I after death invisibly return,
Or, long, long hence, in other spheres,
There to some group of mates the chants resuming,
(Tallying Earth's soil, trees, wind, tumultuous waves).

Ever with pleased smile I may keep on,
Ever and ever yet the verses owning—as, first, I here and now, Signing for Soul and Body,
set to them my name,"

—Walt Whitman, Dedication to *Leaves of Grass*

We can sum up the composition of a sentence in relation to its structure in a picture metaphorically expressed through the human soul life and bodily form, for language is a definite soul movement taking place in a definite bodily form, namely that of Man.

Word
Phrase
Clause
Sentence

PHRASES

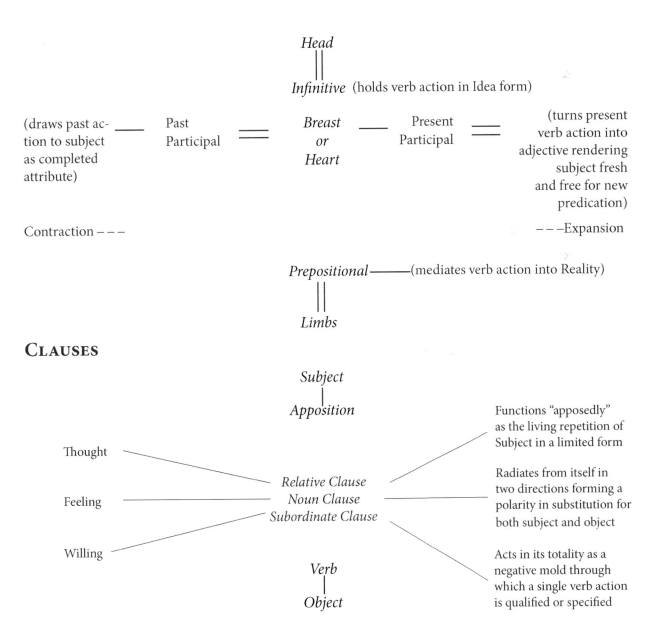

Head

Infinitive (holds verb action in Idea form)

(draws past action to subject as completed attribute) ——— Past Participal ——— *Breast or Heart* ——— Present Participal ——— (turns present verb action into adjective rendering subject fresh and free for new predication)

Contraction – – –   – – –Expansion

Prepositional———(mediates verb action into Reality)

Limbs

CLAUSES

Subject

Apposition

Thought

Feeling

Willing

Relative Clause
Noun Clause
Subordinate Clause

Functions "apposedly" as the living repetition of Subject in a limited form

Radiates from itself in two directions forming a polarity in substitution for both subject and object

Acts in its totality as a negative mold through which a single verb action is qualified or specified

Verb

Object

25

Chapter III
SENTENCE ORGANISM OR PARTS OF SPEECH

These are the eight parts of speech that build the octave of the Sentence. Every existent word strikes one tone on the scale of speech, is one of these eight parts in the sentence organism:

Noun
> Verb
>> Adjective
>>> Adverb
>>>> Preposition
>>>>> Conjunction
>>>>>> Interjection
>>>>>>> Pronoun

THE NOUN

The noun from the Latin meaning name or designation points to the concept of a thing. It is that element which is born from human thought, not from sense perception. Consequently, it is a word coming to rest in man's consciousness and through man is applied to the objects in the world, of his perception, each signifying many particular percepts:

> tree, river, cloud, animal, plant, stone, man, woman, star, wood, table, book, fire, machine, thought, feeling, process, capacity, organ, truth, unit, town, continent, world, way.

When the noun is directed to a single object or unit, not repeated twice in the universe of things, it is called a proper or personal name and is capitalized:

> Chicago, Friday, Michelangelo, English, The Peraclean Age, Philosophy, Egypt, Mars, The 20th Century, Sante Fe Railway, Turning of the Times, Empire State Building, January, Christmas, Grand Canyon, Lincoln Memorial, The Hanging Gardens of Babylon, The Golden Mean, Schubert's Unfinished Symphony, Faust, The Son of God.

Sun, moon and earth were originally in capitals as proper names.

When any normal uncapitalized noun, not naming a particular person, place, time, event, or thing, is put into capitals, it is thereby personified:

> Everyman, Virtue, Spring, Vanity, Friendship, War, Science, Humanity, Nature, Universe, Fantasy.

The Noun or Name is that word through which the human consciousness brings its perceptions into stillness and form. Through the noun in man, the human being, who in essence is not a static thing, but a moving, streaming, inner life constantly in action, a hollow is formed, a clearing or resting place containing a definite form. This is our consciousness of the object, any object, which the noun gives. In noun consciousness we rest in a form, which in its first and larger sense is the earth itself perceived from the standpoint of the human body. And the region of our head where the nouns as the thoughts or names of things are born likens in its round form and resting place, to the earth globe. Hence in German the noun is called "Hauptwort" (Head-word). Through it our consciousness plants itself firmly upon earth.

The noun is the subject of Comparison and Relation.

COMPARISON

The ending in English for the comparative form is "er." When the pronunciation of the comparative form of a word is too cumbersome, the word "more" is used instead.

> Yonder mountain is higher than that upon which we stand.

> Kant's Philosophy is more complicated than a Chinese puzzle.

The noun is subject to comparison through or in its attributes or properties, i.e. through the "adjectives" modifying it. The noun itself is balanced in Place and Form. But through its attribute it can be smaller, larger, brighter, dimmer, softer, harder, sharper, duller, warmer, colder, lighter, darker, louder, softer, heavier, lighter, sweeter, bitterer, smoother, rougher, taller, shorter, broader, narrower, thicker, thinner, higher, lower, deeper, shallower, stronger, weaker, etc. than others. It rocks in its attributes like the baby in a cradle.

The noun can ascend in attribute to the Superlative Form. In that case the ending "est" or the word "most" is used. Then...

> Yonder mountain is the highest in the country.

> Kant's Philosophy is the most complicated of all the philosophies in the Idealist School.

The Comparison can also become "even keel" and the noun balances with another as equal.

> One is as good as another.

In this case "as" as an Adverb is used. As "as" as an adverb is used here, it should be kept in mind that "as" as conjunction, preposition, and as pronoun also appears in the language, just as often as "as" as adverb and in such form and variety as makes "as" as versatile a word as any as has ever (been) spoken from the lips of man, as such. The negative of the equal form above is, formally,

> One is not so good as another.

Or, in the vernacular,

> One is not as good as another.

In all unequal comparisons the word "than" is used. This can be as Preposition simply:

Aphrodite is more beautiful than Hera and Athena, thought Paris.

or as Conjunction:

Ulysses was far more clever than the Trojans gave him credit for.

Actually the full thought, implied in these comparisons is expressed as follows:

Aphrodite is more beautiful than Hera is beautiful and Athena is beautiful, thought Paris.

Ulysses was far more clever than the Trojans gave him credit for being clever.

We have here a balance (or scale) in the sphere of Quality whereon the one side is the Great (greater), the other side the Small (lesser):

Aphrodite is beautiful	Hera is beautiful
"more"	"less"
Ulysses is clever	Trojans think him clever
"more"	"less"

The word "than" is simultaneously a greater and lesser. In comparing two objects in terms of a Quality (adjectivally or adverbially expressed), the one is always on the Great side, the other on the Small side; only we only speak the one out. Both partake of the Quality, but one is differentiated from the other, and the mode of differentiation is the Great-Small, a movement in the Quality attaching to the compared objects which the word "than" grammatically mediates. Now this qualitative movement is in reality a movement in time, for that which is greater is that into or toward which that which is lesser develops, and that which is lesser is that out of, or from which, that which is greater develops. Hence the qualitative distinction must imply or "presuppose" a movement in time. Consider then the Genius of the Language, who derives (to the frequent confusion even of the English speaking people, we might add) from the same Anglo-Saxon old English word both words "than" and "then"!

Now "then" mediates a movement in time as does "than" the movement in quality. For we say:

He picked up his cane, then he put on his hat, and (then) he parted the house, and (then) he walked to the corner, and (then) he crossed the street, ... etc.

or

He mused over the first picture, and then he mused over the second; he thought the first thought and then he thought the second.

All movement in outer space of world or inner place of soul is in discrete moments, as it were, announced through "then," expressed or implied. And every distinction in Quality conceals a distinction in time, or development, which takes place in time:

If Aphrodite is more beautiful than Hera (is beautiful) then in time through development and metamorphosis, Hera's beauty will increase, and then she will be as beautiful as Aphrodite is beautiful.

This becomes still clearer when we express the truth:

Aphrodite is more beautiful now than she was then, i.e. a "time" ago.

The "than" has gone through the "then," that is to say that the change or metamorphosis (in Quality) has gone through the continuum of time (in earthly space and place of soul), and become a drama therein or real movement in time. This is the case in all Comparison. The concept of the pure metamorphosis in time exists, as the "balancing factor" in all Comparison through Quality.

Qualitative Metamorphosis in time as Real
Movement
—Dramatic Action—

Because of this balancing conjunctive character of the word "than," it is excepted from the clause status and given a unique place in the course and consideration, in the "universe" of the Sentence. The "than sentence" would, if containing its original idea, read:

Aphrodite is more beautiful than Hera is less beautiful than Aphrodite is beautiful.

Write a series of sentences comparing objects and persons according to qualities; and another series in which, as in the above example, one object or person is compared to itself in two distinct moments of time, e.g.

The sun is brighter in rising than it is in setting.

Examples of noun attributes in their natural, comparative, and superlative form are:

high	long	good	less	some	great	beautiful
higher	longer	better	lesser	more	greater	more beautiful
highest	longest	best	least	most	greatest	most beautiful

Change the "comparative" forms of the attributes in the above paragraph back to their natural and into their superlative form. Then employ them all, in at least one of their forms, in a sentence.

RELATION

The noun is the subject of Relation, expressed by the genitive, in English "possessive" form. Each noun is the center of a web of relations:

A man may be the:

head of a family	president of a corporation
father of children	student of art
husband of…	lover of good music and rare wine
uncle of…	customer of a department store
citizen of a country	collector of precious stones
member of a community	observer of nature
employee of a company	owner of a car or house
son of his own father, etc.	

We may therefore speak of:

> a man's family
> a man's wife
> a man's citizenship
> a man's sense of observation, etc.

So we have:

1) The noun as subject of relations outwardly expressed and ordered concentrically around it—formed grammatically with the Possessive "of."

2) The noun as subject of relations inwardly expressed, i.e. expressed as if they were the subject's own attributes formed grammatically with the "s." (When a word already ends in "s" the apostrophe is merely added scissors', blades'.)

Outward	Inward
A citizen of Rome	Rome's citizens

Whether we use the one form or the other is a question of euphony, sentence rhythm, or emphasis:

> Orpheus, the son of Apollo   Orpheus, Apollo's son

Form possessives with the following pairs:

magic – magician	witch – hour	breath – dragon
night – gloom	Satan – hoof	church – might
king – subjects	memories – youth	courage – soldier
Ides – March	sighs – lover	paradise – fool
Raphael – paintings	song – Nightingale	wind – whipping
heaven – canopy	hand – fingers	woman – hair
people – world	destiny – man	bill – doctor
joy – children	eve – midsummer	shore – ocean
sense – life	tail – comet	Pompey – fall

Review

In its "comparative action" the noun is sphere-building. It puts all other things (beings, objects) into the distance of great(er) and less(er), expands centrifugally out of its own self, and rests in the balance or equality of its own being. Therefore it creates its own sphere qualitatively and has its own time. It nulls the world, creating its own "hollow" therein.

In its "relating (possessing) action" the noun centripetally refers all things to itself, as of so many concentric spheres about it, each of different magnitude and order, building a possessing middle point round which they revolve. Hence it "fills" the hollow with the fullness of all things in existence to itself.

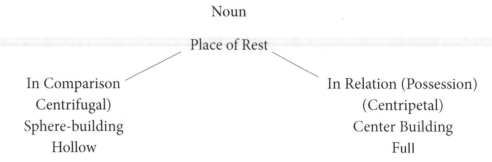

Noun

Place of Rest

In Comparison   In Relation (Possession)
Centrifugal)   (Centripetal)
Sphere-building   Center Building
Hollow   Full

THE VERB

The verb, (Latin, *Verbum*: literally, "word) is the Alpha and Omega, of all language, its source and bloom, what we have in the beginning:

"In the beginning was the Word" (—as Cause)

—St. John

and what we have in the end:

In the end is the Word—as goal.

The Verb is a process or movement beginning in action and ending in existence (manifestation) with a midway state of action + existence or possession. Therefore the three major verbs in any language from which all other verbs are derived are:

To Do   —   Action
To Have   —   Possession
To Be   —   Existence

All action tends to existence and all existence tends to act. To illustrate, consider the artist or musician. He begins practicing his instrument, mere action, full of squeaks and squawks. After a few years he *has* a little skill and practices a little more. Finally, after may years he *is* a musician. What is his action now? The same: playing his instrument; but now the action is manifestation of being, namely of the accomplished artist, not the activity of becoming, i.e. of the musician to be.

All verbs, excepting "to have" and "to be," are actions subsumable under the Genus "to do." Therefore in German the verb is called *Tunwort* ("Do-word"). As, in the consideration of the noun, all Forms are at rest in Place, so, respecting the Verb, we can say all action, all *doing*, is in movement in Time.

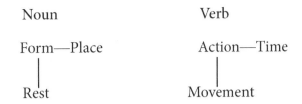

	Noun		Verb
	Form—Place		Action—Time
	Rest		Movement

Time is centered in the human Self, which experiences before and after. Its essence is the "I" incorporated. The Ego Presence in the body thus builds the beginning point of the human sense of time: the Present Tense (tense from Latin *tempus* = time).

PRESENT TENSE

As an Ego, Self, or I, present in the body, man can look backward and forward. Hence from the Present we derive the:

Past Tense and Future Tense.

The Present, Past, and Future Tense of the three major verbs are:

I do	We do
You do	You do
He, she, it does	They do

I did	We did	I shall do	We shall do
You did	You did	You will do	You will do
He, she, it did	They did	He, she, it will do	They will do

What I do, I did and shall do

I have	We have
You have	You have
He, she, it has	They have

I had	We had	I shall have	We shall have
You had	You had	You will have	You will have
He, she, it had	They had	He, she, it will have	They will have

What I have, I had and shall have

I am	We are
You are	You are
He, she, it is	They are

I was	We were	I shall be	We shall be
You were	You were	You will be	You will be
He, she, it was	They were	He, she, it will be	They will be

What I am, I was and shall be

In addition to these "irregular" verbs, the three fundamental tenses of a "regular" verb are formed as follows:

To walk:	I walk	We walk
	You walk	You walk
	He, she, it walks	They walk

I walked	We walked	I shall walk	We shall walk
You walked	You walked	You will walk	You will walk
He, she, it walked	They walked	He, she, it will walk	They will walk

The **Present Tense** for all regular and all irregular verbs excepting "to be" is formed by using the verb stem (infinitive without the "to"). In the third person singular an "s" is added, an "es" in the case of verbs such as go and do.

The **Past Tense** for all regular verbs is formed by added "*ed*" to the verb stem in certain cases after doubling the last consonant: rap(ped), tap(ped), trip(ped), rip(ped), et.al. The form thus attained remains the same for all persons singular and plural. This latter is also true of all irregular verbs in the Past Tense (e.g. "had" and "did" above) excepting "to be."

The **Future Tense** for all verbs regular and irregular is formed by adding to the verb stem the auxiliary "*shall*" in the first persons, "*will*" in the second and third persons. When emphasizing the will force in decisions for the future these auxiliaries are exactly reversed:

> "This I do vow, and this shall ever be.
> I will be true, despite thy scythe and thee."
> —Shakespeare, Sonnet 123

In addition to the fundamental movement in time through Present, Past and Future Tense, there exist the "**Perfect**" Tenses.

Present Perfect

Past Perfect

Future Perfect

These tenses are formed by combining the past participle of the verb with the verb "to have," used as auxiliary in this formation. We need but repeat the present, past, and future of "to have" as given above, adding the past participle in each instance. Example: done, past participle of "to do."

	I have done	We have done
	You have done	You have done
	He, she it has done	They have done

I had done	We had done	I shall have done	We shall have done
You had done	You had done	You will have done	You will have done
He, she, it had done	They had done	He, she, it will have done	They will have done

It is important to properly distinguish the three perfect tenses from the three prime tenses.

In the three prime tenses—present, past, future—time is "infinite." Its movement occurs under the aspect of eternity. Consider:

"The moving finger writes and having writ moves on."
—Omar Khayam

The ocean swells.

Man breathes.

I love.

These statements in the Present have no limit, they are expressed as eternal truths. The time or moment of their signifying power is not finite, but infinite.

When I direct myself to the Past, it stretches backward infinitely. I can read it as an infinite record of event. Each fact, each experience, each deed whether done yesterday, a thousand years ago, or at Creation's beginning, lies open to scrutiny and twinkles as one star in the vast canopy of the heavens, stretched, in this case, a starry robe, flowing as a wake into the endless past. Out of this Infinite Record I say, e.g.:

Washington crossed the Delaware on Christmas night in the winter of 1776.

"First there was Chaos, the vast immeasurable abyss,
Outrageous as a sea, dark, wasteful, wild."
—Milton

John baptized Jesus.

Egypt reached its height of development in the 14th century B.C. through the figure of King Amenophis IV: Ihknaton.

Yesterday we dined alone.

So in the Future tense does time stretch infinitely before us. What limits can be set to the will, to the "I shall!" Time lies open infinitely futureward. And any expression of the future tense is into this unending Forward.

"I shall be with you always even unto the end of the world." —Matthew

"Mine appetite I never more will grind
On newer proof, to try an older friend,
A god in love, to whom I am confined."
—Shakespeare

"Even this shall pass away."— Eastern Proverb

With the Perfect Tenses, time is made "finite," because it is fixed at a definite point in the Past, at a definite point in the Future, and completed in the Present.

The people in the colonies had had little common matter for conversation before Benjamin Franklin began circulating "Poor Richard's Almanac."

She had grown in stature and beauty since his last visit.

There is a definite point referred to the Past. The Past Perfect records the time up to this point. Hence in German it is called "*Vorvergangenheit*"—before (a definite point in) the past. The time, thus limited, is finite. The case is the same with the Future Perfect.

By next October we shall have lived in Europe thirteen years.

An Important Distinction:

The Present Perfect Tense is not equivalent to the Past Tense in English, nor can it in any way be a substitute of the Past, as is possible, and practiced in German. By using the Present Perfect we do one of two things:

a) either we complete an action up into the present, carry it from some point in the past into the present, whereby it is not discontinued, though rendered finite in the present moment.

He has played tennis ever since he learned it in college.

She has always possessed a clear sense of logic.

b) or we take an event out of the past, a star from the flowing robe of past experience and hold it up to view, pin it on our breast like a general's metals:

I have seen a ghost!

Tenzing has climbed every major mountain in the Himalayas. They have often been to Italy, but never to Rome.

She has just finished preparing lunch.

These sentences should be radically distinguished from the same events merely recorded in the Past Tense:

I saw a ghost.

Tenzing climbed every major mountain in the Himalayas.

They often went to Italy, but never to Rome.

She just finished preparing lunch.

The latter (past) tense narrates and describes a fact, finished and done, reads it in the infinite robe of the past. The Present Perfect tense lifts this fact into the present and expresses it as something special, as a true "possession."

Do you see this hand?

This hand has shaken the hand of a man who shook the hand of another man who shook the hand of Abraham Lincoln!

Once the revelation is given in the Present perfect tense, then, of course, the prosaic description follows in the past tense, e.g.:

In Present Perfect:

The first human being has just landed on the Sun!

In the Simple Past:

The first human being, a citizen of the whole world, landed yesterday in the newest and most perfect spaceship, "Born Innocent," after a most daring and dangerous approach through the famous Flaming Portal of her sunny side in close range to the Muses' Fountain of Fire, on the Sun, that nearest of the fixed stars in our galaxy, just as she rose in the heat of her Day Radiance, thereby becoming the first earthly creature to get the "inside story" on the life of the universe. He was honored as a hero, feasted generously, presented with the Metal of the Golden Heart for courage and wisdom, and a first edition copy of the book "Art of Sunshining," given twelve full baskets of pure light containing sunbeams from dawn, morning, noon, afternoon, and dusk, a vial containing that most exquisite of elixirs "Solar Essence" to ward off cold drafts on the return trip, and with a revolving invitation to come at any time again, was cheered off with a new Song of Cosmic Love in one hundred and forty four part spherical harmony, as his ship, sun-washed and re-christened "Become Wise," took wing back to the earth.

So:

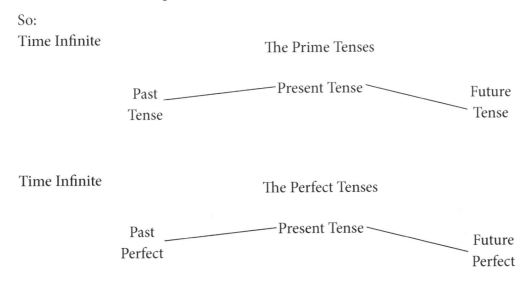

Write the equivalent sentences in the Past Tense of the following sentences in the Present Perfect, adding the necessary descriptive modifiers to paint the full picture.

He has faced a man-eating tiger in the jungle interior of Africa.

She has swum the English Channel.

We have driven from Ankara to Edinburgh by car.

Our good friends have just bought a house.

An earthquake has recently destroyed a village of 5,000 inhabitants in the heart of Mexico.

Air transportation has forced the giant ocean liners out of business.

The birds have flown south for the winter.

The first fashions of the season have already appeared in the store windows.

The President has returned from China.

The verbs "to be" and "to have" in the Perfect Tenses conjugate as follows:

To have:

I have had	We have had
You have had	You have had
He, she it has had	They have had

I had had	We had had	I shall have had	We shall have had
You had had	You had had	You will have had	You will have had
He, she, it had had	They had had	He, she, it will have had	They will have had

What I had had, have had, shall have had, I have.

To be:

I have been	We have been
You have been	You have been
He, she it has been	They have been

I had been	We had been	I shall have been	We shall have been
You had been	You had been	You will have been	You will have been
He, she, it had been	They had been	He, she, it will have been	They will have been

What I had been, have been, shall have been, I am.

CONTINUOUS FORM

The English Language, as excepted among all languages, has developed the Continuous or "ing" Form of the Verb in all its tenses. To construct this Form we use the verb "to be" as auxiliary and add "ing" to the verb stem, thus forming the present participle"

to act	—acting
to lie	—lying
to live	—living
to try	—trying
to nap	—napping
to rustle	—rustling
to flit	—flitting

Example: to live. Add the present participle living to the forms of "to be" above.

Prime Tenses:

I am living	We are living
You are living	You are living
He, she it is living	They are living

I was living	We were living	I shall be living	We shall be living
You were living	You were living	You will be living	You will be living
He, she, it was living	They were living	He, she, it will be living	They will be living

Perfect Tenses:

I have been living	We have been living
You have been living	You have been living
He, she, it has been living	They have been living

I had been living   We had been living
You had been living   You had been living
He, she, it had been living   They had been living

I shall have been living   We shall have been living
You will have been living   You will have been living
He, she, it will have been living   They will have been living

The "ing" form of the verb is as a window out of which one gazes into the immediacy of life and a direct perception or event, whereas the regular "simple" form of the verbs mediates that same life and event in the form of thought or the concept. An example in the Present Tense may serve to illustrate.

> The sun is rising

is a direct perception experienced in the moment or now.

Actually the full expression, always implicit when using the Continuous Form is:

> Look (or See), the sun is rising!

"The sun is rising" is something immediately perceived—a Percept.

Now consider the Simple Form of Present Tense:

> The sun rises.

By itself, thus formulated, this sentence is a dead form, a pure abstraction, never spoken, never expressed. To have meaning and be a real sentence in a living context it must have modifiers that set it into actuality:

> The sun rises every day in the morning at a definite time which varies throughout the year.

By the same token it now is not a percept or observation, but a Concept, a conceived fact or thought which is valid for all times.

Thus the distinction between the normal verb tenses and the continuos verb tenses accurately seen is the distinction between Concept and Percept.

Simple Verb Form   Continuous Verb Form

Concept   Percept

The same may be illustrated through use of any other tense. Take the Past Tense. Consider the following text.

> They started their mountain climb early. They walked through the woods and followed the trails up to the low slopes. At the monastery they had lunch. Then they continued up the higher slopes and finally reached the top around three o'clock in the afternoon. It was a beautiful view from up there. The air was clear and a light wind was blowing. While fluffy clouds were drifting slowly across the blue sky, the golden yellow of the sun was glistening upon the peaks of the thousand cliffs that could be seen from this enchanted spot. Bird

songs were wafting up from the valley below. An eagle on the wing was swaying slowly on the edge of a neighboring mountain. And it seemed that the whole of nature was breathing forth a transparency like that of dew on Creation's first morn. Then they descended, took five hours making their way down, and arrived at their hut in the forest just as the last red-rose rays of the setting sun were streaming in dreamy haze through the leafy branches of the trees.

Here is to begin with a narration of a sequence of past actions, a mere recording of completed events in conceptual form using the simple **Past Tense**:

> They started, they walked, followed, had lunch, continued, reached. It was a beautiful view, the air was.

Up to this point we have recorded the thought or memory picture of what happened on the mountain climb. At this junction, however, we break the narrative to express an "immediate moment of perception" experienced on the climb. We are not thinking the past action now, but are again in the moment of perceiving what on the mountain top we perceived. Hence we change to the Continuous ("ing") Form of the verb:

> Clouds were drifting, sun was glistening, bird songs were wafting, an eagle was swaying, all of nature was breathing…

Now the narrative continues with the concept of the rest of the outing, again merely recording the completed past action, until at the very end another "window" is opened in the memory through which, while in the past tense, we look, as we did then, into the forest and "see" what is happening in the moment, namely, the sun's rays streaming though the branches, which we therefore express in the Past Continuous.

Practice writing simple narratives in the Past Tense and try thereby to develop a feeling for the distinction between a mere description of a course of actions or events and a window that opens up in the midst of these events to record (express) an actual Perceiving or Seeing done in the past.

THREEFOLD NOW

The "Moment" in which human consciousness lives when in the Continuous Form is threefold, again best illustrated through the **Present Tense**:

1) The Absolute Moment— what I actually perceive happening right now with my senses: Can you hear the town crier crying: "Ten o'clock and all's well"?

2) The World Moment— what is happening at the moment in the world beyond my actual sense perception, but perceived imaginatively as a logical extension thereof:

> The house wives in New York are preparing coffee (while we are just shutting off the light for bed).

3) The Life Moment— what happens in a certain period of life which can be regarded as an extended moment:

> John is studying at the university. He just started and shall be going for the next four years.

At the moment she's working as a stewardess for American Airlines. She's been one for seven years now.

The formulations in the Continuous Form are always made from the standpoint of Perception, not of Thought.

We have been attending lectures for over twelve years... I see this, looking back, and express my perception. Otherwise I would state the mere fact (thought):

We have attended lectures for over twelve years.

In either case, however, the action "attending" still exists, still is going on. Only when I say:

We attended lectures for over twelve years

using the **Past Tense** (simple) do I state that the action is completed, that we no longer attend lectures.

Examples:

Perception	Thought (Fact or Concept)
The birds are singing. (I hear them)	The birds sing every morning. (a fact)
The stars were shining last night. (I saw them)	The stars shone brightly last night. (a recorded fact)
The leaves will be turning soon. (I can see them in my fantasy)	The leaves will turn in October. (according to fact)
They've been living across the street for years. (I see back over the years)	They have lived across the street for years. (factual statement)
We had been working hard in the fields before the rains came. (I see it in the past)	We had worked hard in the fields before the rains came. (a fact)
By the age of twenty he shall have been playing the piano 11 years. (this I picture in front of me)	By the age of twenty he shall have played the piano 11 years. (fact deduced)

Change the following Concepts to Percepts, i.e. verbs in the simple to verbs in the continuous form, thereby dropping the modifiers when necessary:

Always ask: what is the pure perception?

Example:

The wind blows strongly in these parts. (A fact or concept recorded or told)	The wind is blowing strongly. (A perception while actually present "in these parts")

Roses bloom in summer.

The mists rise after the sun goes down.

They fish in the wee hours of the morn.

The actors perform in the park for the public on Sundays.

The wind blew wildly on the day they set sail.

Last Christmas snow fell.

Our guests will stay for the weekend.

She has practiced cello all afternoon.

Change the following Perceptions to thoughts, that is, put the "ing"-form sentences in their simple form, adding the appropriate modifiers to form a living concept in a real context, not just an abstract form.
Always ask: what is the concept?
Example:

The robins are building their nests (It is spring).

The robins build their nests every spring (in the spring).

Halley's Comet will soon be coming again.

The squirrels are already beginning to gather nuts for winter.

Our whole Age is pondering over evil, as the Greek Age pondered over death.

They're having breakfast on the verandah.

The issue is being discussed in the House at this very moment.

In California the orange trees are blossoming.

He had been reading late in his study when suddenly he heard a knocking at the door.

Practice writing sentences in these two forms, Regular or Simple and Continuous, in all tenses, till you develop a "sense" or feeling for the difference. Only thus can it be learned.

Passive Voice

Verbs can be in the Passive Voice as well as the Active Voice. The Passive Voice in English is also formed, like the Continuous Form, by using the verb "to be" as auxiliary. To it is added the Past Participle. Consider "to carry," Past participle: Carried:

I am carried	We are carried
You are carried	You are carried
He, she it is carried	They are carried

I was carried	We were carried	I shall be carried	We shall be carried
You were carried	You were carried	You will be carried	You will be carried
He, she, it was carried	They were carried	He, she, it will be carried	They will be carried

I have been carried	We have been carried
You have been carried	You have been carried
He, she it has been carried	They have been carried

I had been carried	We had been carried
You had been carried	You had been carried
He, she, it had been carried	They had been carried

I shall have been carried	We shall have been carried
You will have been carried	You will have been carried
He, she, it will have been carried	They will have been carried

The full concept of Passivity and Activity (Passive and Active Voice) respecting verb action involves the transposition of the object to the subject, and the subject to the object.

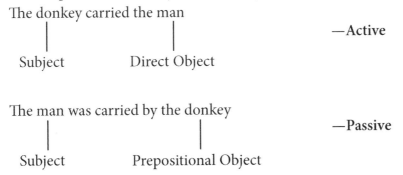

For this transposition the preposition "by" is used. The Passive need not express its object as does the Active. One can say simply:

The man was carried.

Change the following into Passive Voice:

The company consumed the whole soup in one sitting.

He had driven his car ten times ten thousand miles before he junked it.

The wind blew the clouds in large masses across the sky.

Johanna tended the garden with care.

Each student spoke the poem by heart.

The jockeys checked all the horses before the race began.

The cameramen shot the scene twice to make sure of a take.

Put the following into the Active Voice:

She will be taken to the hospital by an ambulance.

Rome has often been sacked by invaders.

He was nursed back to life by a devoted friend.

Constantinople was founded by Constantine.

"All Gaul is divided into three parts."

Elizabeth was loved by Essex more than she loved him.

He had been borne to earth on a beam of light.

QUESTION AND NEGATION

Both Question Form and Negation Form in English use "to do" as auxiliary verb with all verbs except "to be" and "to have."

Question	Answer
Do you like home-made peach pie warm from the oven, with a dip of ice-cream along with it?	I love home-made peach pie warm from the oven- ala mode.
Did the Pied Piper of Hamlin succeed in cleaning the city of the rats?	The Pied Piper of Hamlin did succeed in cleaning the city of the rats, and of the children, too.
Has Agnis made the beds with hospital with corners?	Yes, Agnis has made the beds, but not with hospital corners.

Statement	Negation
Napoleon won the battle of Waterloo.	Napoleon did not win the battle of Waterloo.
Man has descended from the animal.	Man has not descended from the animal, the animal has descended from man.

With the verb "to be" the Question is formed merely by reversing the position of the subject and verb, as is the case with all questions in German:

Statement	Question
They are at home.	Are they at home?
Today is the longest day of the year.	Is today the longest day of the year?
Aristotle was Plato's pupil.	Was Aristotle Plato's pupil?

Statement	Negation
Socrates was French.	Socrates was not French.
The Atlantic is the world's largest ocean.	The world's largest ocean is not the Atlantic, it is the Pacific.
The price of milk has remained the same.	The price of milk has not remained the same., it has gone up.

With the verb "to have" the Question and Negation can be formed both ways:

Question	Negation
Has he a villa in Spain?	He has not (hasn't) a villa in Spain.
Does he have a villa in Spain?	He doesn't have a villa in Spain.

An Aside:

A colloquial form of Question and Negation, particularly favored by the British, who love speaking in the back of the throat, but actually incorrect grammatically, being a redundancy, is:

> Has he got a bit of horse sense?   He hasn't got a bit of horse sense.

Got is the past (participle) of get which means "to acquire or fetch." Here, however, the sense is that of "possessing," which the verb "has" also expresses. Hence, the meaning doubles:

> Has he got = possesses he (the) possessed

If "has" is to act merely as an auxiliary verb, then got must mean possessed as participle:

> Has he got = has he possessed

which is not what the phrase conveys in ordinary usage. Since both possibilities "possesses he possessed," and "has he possessed" are incorrect grammatically or from the standpoint of what meaning the words actually convey, the phrase can only be explained as follows:

> Has he got? = Does he have?

And therefore, since it actually means Does he have?, it is far less complicated, far more proper grammatically, certainly primary, and also better sounding to form the Question and Negation in the English language, straight down the line, with "to do."

EMPHASIS

A further usage of "to do" as auxiliary verb is for emphasis in affirming a statement. The emphatic affirmative is usually occasioned by a denial:

> They were in London but they didn't see the Queen.

> They did see the Queen. <or> They did too see the Queen. <or> They certainly did see the Queen.

First change to questions, then negate, then reaffirm emphatically.

> The Spanish Armada was vanquished by the English Navy under Elizabeth I.

> Rudyard Kipling wrote a poem entitled "IF."

> Hamburgers taste best with fried onions.

> Bronco Nagurski was a fullback for the Chicago Bears.

> Babe Ruth still holds the all time baseball record for home runs.

> The Nicene Creed was written in 329 in Nicea as the result of a church controversy concerning the nature of the persons of the Trinity.

> There is no external historical reason why the Mongols halted before the doors of Europe, since nothing earthly could have prevented the hordes from exterminating the whole of it.

> Children have always hated going to the dentist.

> He shall have been fighting over three hours by the time he lands that fish. We had to change clothes for dinner.

They love each other dearly.

We can now, in review, see how the three major verbs "to do," "to have," and "to be," like three great generals in the field, are used in their "auxiliary" role to affect the action of all verb usage:

To Do—used to form the Question and the Negation, or in Emphatic Affirmation

To Have—used to form the Perfect Tenses

To Be—used to form the Passive Voice and the Continuous Form of the Verb

REVIEW OF VERB

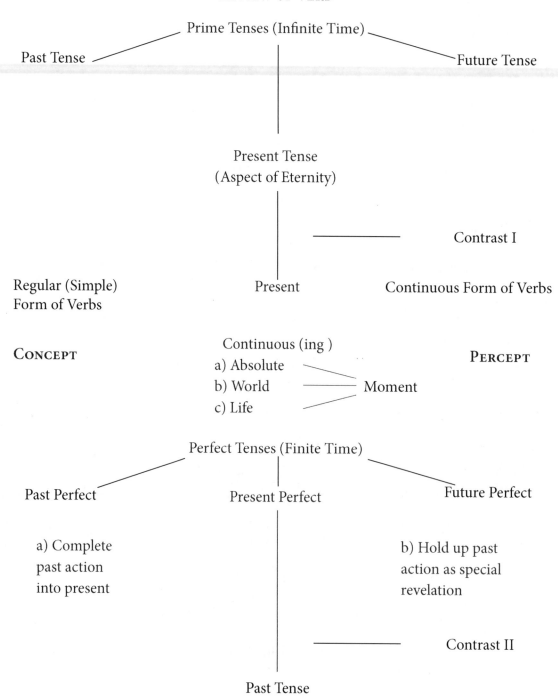

Prime Tenses (Infinite Time)

Past Tense   Future Tense

Present Tense
(Aspect of Eternity)

Contrast I

Regular (Simple)   Present   Continuous Form of Verbs
Form of Verbs

CONCEPT   Continuous (ing)   **PERCEPT**
a) Absolute
b) World   Moment
c) Life

Perfect Tenses (Finite Time)

Past Perfect   Present Perfect   Future Perfect

a) Complete   b) Hold up past
past action   action as special
into present   revelation

Contrast II

Past Tense

THE ADJECTIVE

The word "adjective" comes from the Latin word "*jicere*" meaning to throw and the prefix "ad" meaning to, at, next to. In German it is called "*Eigenschaftswort*" (Attribute Word) or "*Fiihlwort*" (Feeling Word). It modifies only the noun. A series of common adjectives are:

light — dark	critical — kind
bold — modest	fair — foul
generous — stingy	caustic — mellow
ripe — green	fat — skinny
gay — blue	honest — crafty
prompt — late	slender — obese
rash — considerate	begun — finished
pure — tainted	famous —unknown
true — false	spirited — deflated
right —wrong	courageous — cowardly
lovable — hateful	friendly — mean
hesitant — hasty	vacillating — unswerving
happy — sad	unprejudiced — bias
sorrowful — joyful	victorious — vanquished
real— ideal	forthright — sneaky
wild — serene	pleasant — nasty
impassioned — pacific	filthy — clean
clear — muddled	nervous — relaxed
interesting — boring	mild — harsh
curious — indifferent	full — empty
wise — foolish	frequent — seldom
witty — dull	rare — common

As the noun expresses how human thought brings to rest in a named image (object) the world movement,

> "You objects that call from diffusion my meanings and give them shape."
> —Walt Whitman

and the verb gives immediate expression to this movement, **which is prime and prior to the noun,** the Adjectives express the human soul reaction to the objects of the world brought into form and place by human thought. Therefore they express, as do also the adverbs in relation to verbs, the characteristic of this soul life, namely the alternating rhythm between sympathy and antipathy. An adjective is always in a contrast or polarity to another adjective signifying the opposite—that the human soul has in it the possibility of a dual reaction to all conceived objects, events, and experiences in life and the world, this fact is reflected grammatically in the language by the usage of the Adjective in modifying the noun.

There are three forms of adjectival modification, for the adjective can be a word, a phrase, or a clause.

WORD —
the little lake
the little lake in the chain

PHRASE —
the little lake in the chain lying so still
the little lake in the chain lying so still surrounded by pine trees

CLAUSE —
the little lake in the chain, which we loved so dearly in our youth,
lying so still surrounded by tall dark pines.

Note: as mentioned in Chapter II, the prepositional phrase can be used both as adjective and adverb; the participial phrases are always adjectives, though sometimes adverbial in emphasis or position; but the relative clause is only adjectival.

As a word or phrase the adjective can be put after the verb (in the predicate) as well:
Life is worth living.

The sky has been cloudy these past few days.

This is only the case with the verb "to be," however, since in such sentences as:
The cake tastes delicious

"delicious" is an adverb. A noun can also be used adjectivally in English:
those good old horse and buggy days

ski boots and swimming suits

United States Steel

the Michael Age

Typical adjectival endings in English are:

able (ible) — possible, capable, noticeable, readable
al — partial, hypocritical, musical, immortal
ed — charged, sure—footed, sacred, colored
ful — playful, helpful, bashful, bountiful
ant (ent) — brilliant, pursuant, mordant, abundant
ile — docile, volatile, fertile
ic — caustic, tragic, comic, romantic
ish — squeamish, bluish, fiendish
y — muggy, dreamy, cranky
ous — numerous, beauteous, perilous, marvelous
ate (ite) — fortunate, compassionate, incommensurate
less — ruthless, fearless, harmless
like — warlike, lionlike, lifelike

The common form of adjectival opposition (contrast or negation) is through "un," or "in," or "non."

> conscious — unconscious
> sufficient — insufficient
> existent — nonexistent

The "comparative" manifestation of the Adjective was discussed in Chapter II. All articles (a, an, the) and numbers (ordinal and cardinal) are adjectives: everything that limits or defines the noun.

THE ADVERB

The Adverb is the "Jack of All Trades" among the Parts of Speech. It can modify every word but the noun. While the Adjective, variable in quality as it is, confines its modifying skill and attention strictly to the Noun, the Adverb is the all around athlete who helps every word in its turn:

Cheetah runs swiftly.	—modifying the Verb
'Tis a frightfully hot day.	—modifying the Adjective
Most mightily did the breakers roar against the rocks.	—modifying the Adverb
Far down in the valley the herd of horses could be seen.	—modifying the Preposition
Even though the tide was coming in, he risked rowing to the island.	—modifying the conjunction
Well, by George, I'm game!	—modifying the Interjection

In its favorite role as modifier of the Verb, the Adverb has likewise three forms: it can be a single word, a phrase, or a clause:

> The peacock slowly spread open the feathers of its tail. —Word

> With a graceful swing, accompanied by a shrill proclamation, the peacock spread open its tail feathers. —Phrase

> While all the bystanders gaped in amazement, the peacock spread wide its splendid tail until it formed a full and radiant thousand-eyed fan. — Clause

Note: the prepositional phrase is used as adverb as well as adjective; but the subordinate clause is always and only adverbial.

As the noun is the subject of comparison through its attributes (the Adjective) so is the Verb through the Adverb.

> Porthos fenced well.

> Athos fenced better than the rest

> D'Artagan fenced the best of all the Musketeers.

In form the Adverb is for the most part an adjective with "ly" added to it.

> "I coughed gently and apologetically. I coughed upbraidingly, sorrowfully, suggestively, authoritatively, meekly, imperiously, agreeably, hopefully, hopelessly, despairingly, and quite vainly."—Christopher Wren, *Beau Geste*

In some cases the same word in positive, comparative, and superlative is both.

As Adjective	**As Adverb**
deep water	dived deep
deeper water	dived deeper
deepest water	dived deepest

However the Adverb can also be formulated:

deeply

more deeply

most deeply

Examples of such Adjective—Adverb words are:

slow	smooth	loose	much	straight
fast	rough	tight	hard	close
high	right	early	fair	bad
low	wrong	late	sharp	bright

The Adjective and the Adverb are thus like twins, the one content to remain at home with the Noun, in peace by the hearthside, manifesting itself usefully and colorfully in a million ways; the other anxious to rove the fields and lands, woods and lakes of the Sentence's mighty estates, accompanying the Verb on all its travels, visiting in turn the abodes and dwellings of all the parts of speech, serving each with its manifold and remarkable ability to characterize and create, the one still, the other ever in motion the one central, the other circumferential; the one holding to the fulcrum, pivotal point or balance in the sentence, where the noun is at rest in place, the other constantly in movement with the verb in time, circulating throughout the sentence; each manifesting in the dual form of:

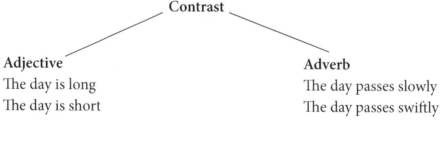

Contrast

Adjective	**Adverb**
The day is long	The day passes slowly
The day is short	The day passes swiftly

each performing the:

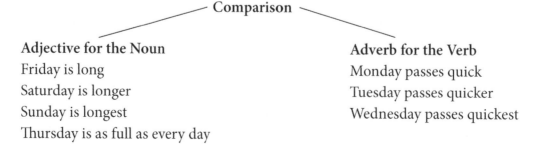

Comparison

Adjective for the Noun	**Adverb for the Verb**
Friday is long	Monday passes quick
Saturday is longer	Tuesday passes quicker
Sunday is longest	Wednesday passes quickest
Thursday is as full as every day	

each capable of the threefold form of:

Modification

	Adjective	**Adverb**
Word—	The barn is red	Corn grows tall
Phrase—	There is a red barn with a silver silo!	Corn grows with golden kernels and a brown beard.
Clause—	The red barn with the silver silo on one end, which is so characteristic of the Midwest American country side is a simplified version on the economic plane of the European cathedral.	Corn grows best where the soil is sandy and the sun hot.

THE PREPOSITION

The best way to understand the preposition is to imagine that we are living in a sea of warmth, differentiated in endless varying degrees, but a warmth that is not a state or condition, but rather "pure will." Man's every movement, of body, soul, or spirit, is prepositioned Noun, modulated in and through this Will. I lift my hand up, point it at, draw it down, place it upon, offer it to, put it into, take it out of, wrap the fingers around, hold something between them, point it at, push the hand through a coat sleeve, turn it over, put it under, above, next to, behind, in front of, etc. A thousand objects continuously the same with the movement of arms, legs, head, feet, shoulders, body as a whole, eyes. I look at, upon, over, under, on the right, on the left, up, down, through, between, for, after, before, around, about, within, as far as, beside, until, to, from, in, beyond, below, etc. constantly. In every living waking instant my whole being, body, soul and spirit is by its verb action differentiating, modulating this element of Will, which conceived in its differentiation or crystallized out, as it were, into directional and positional units of Meaning, into words that signify the direction or position of the Verb action in relation to its Noun (Object), is the Preposition. Imagine a seemingly solid mass of water that actually consists of a multitude of single, individual drops. So Man, or any subject moving through the sea of will or life whose expression grammatically is "Prepositions"! Their function is dual:

Prepositions express the Element of Will or Life

through which the Verb moves towards its object: here it is	in which the Noun exists as Object: here it is
Direction	**Position**
Example: He walked into the garden.	Example: The garden was near the city.
as Adverb	as Adjective

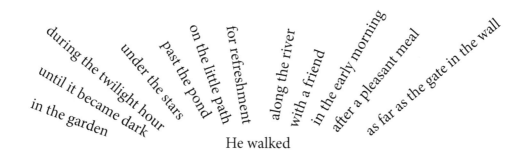

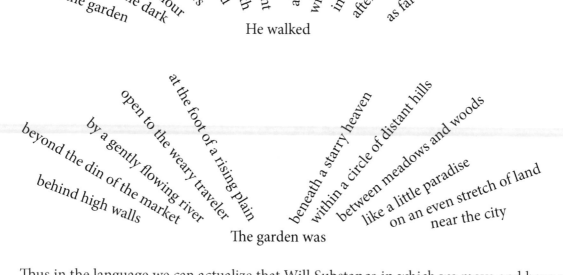

Thus in the language we can actualize that Will Substance in which we move and have our being into Phrases or Units of Meaning that render us conscious of the Adverbial Sense of (our) movement and the Adjectival Sense of (our) being.

The Preposition can also follow an adjective:

Weary with toil, he took to his bed.

Rich in imagination and old in experience, he set out to write his Revelations.

They heard the news jumping for joy.

Such phrases are, however, built on the same principle and in the same form as the Participial Phrase, which, in its more complete form, is also adjective + prepositional phrase:

Present Participial
normal
"jumping wildly"

Present Participial
complete (with prepositional phrase)
"jumping for joy"

Past Participial
normal
"markedly aged"

Past Participial
complete
"aged by experience"

Hence the Preposition and its Phrase remain twin in sense, signification, and use.

Write sentences using the following prepositions:

Apropos	in regard to
in spite of	referring to
by virtue of	with respect to
in view of	concerning

via	past
per	except (but)
on account of	onto
because of	as to
according to	in accordance with
contrary to	according to
throughout	by means of
without	due to
up to	apart from
alongside	unto
as a result of	instead of
since	inside
ahead of	toward
besides	in place of

THE CONJUNCTION

Up to this point we have considered five parts of speech

Noun   Verb

Adjective   Adverb

Preposition

and have seen how they interrelate in the Sentence—the Noun and Verb, those two mighty opposites, ever at rest, ever in motion, building in cooperation the foundational components (Subject and Verb) of the Sentence; the Adjective ever faithful to the noun, ever at work in its aura, who can so identify itself with the Noun, that it can mark off in the rhythmic stride of the relative clause the fullness of its meaning; the Adverb, twin brother of the Adjective, convoy to the Verb in all action marking off through the subordinate clause the single shades of qualification surrounding it, ever at work throughout the whole universe of the Sentence, in all its spheres (parts) but that of the Noun; and the Preposition, dynamic expression of the dual nature of Adjective-Adverb in the deeper element of the Sentence Life or Will. Now, the Conjunction.

There are only three major conjunctions in any tongue, of which the first is:

"And"

the second

"But"

and the third

"Or"

with its negative

"Nor."

All other conjunctions are "subordinate conjunctions" introducing subordinate clauses which we have treated in Chapter II. "For" is a subordinate conjunction like "because," the latter, a shortened

form of "by the cause of" giving the causal connection, the former giving the "reason" not the cause for a deed, e.g.:

> He went along on the Safari, for he thought he might discover some diamond mines.

> They organized the Safari because they wanted to hunt the wild elephant.

Words such as:

> therefore, consequently, however, meanwhile, thus, truly, moreover,

whether modifying the whole sentence or a part are in principle adverbs, not conjunctions. A conjunction (Latin: *junctio* = to join, *con* = with) joins

> Sentences
>
> Clauses
>
> Phrases
>
> Words

The sentence is a movement of the soul. Just as the movement of the body as a whole is called "walking" and consists of lifting the foot of the leg from the earth, carrying it for a length approximately three times as long as the foot, and then placing the foot again upon the earth, so the movement of the soul, expressed as a whole in the sentence, is the movement from Subject through Verb to Object.

Bodily Movement: Walking	Soul Movement: Speaking
Lift	Subject
Carry	Verb
Place	Object

Now, the "sentencing" of the speaking soul, the movement i.e. from sentence to sentence takes place in a threefold way:

> first as an   Or
>
> then as a   But
>
> and finally as   And

Just as we constantly come to crossroads while walking and must decide to go one way or the other, so that every straight path is really the result of a definite decision, so in acting, the human will is first confronted with the crossroad:

> This much is to tell—he shall become a doctor and heal men or he shall study music and compose new symphonies.

> "Give me Liberty or give me death."
>
>   —Patrick Henry

Once the decision is made, the great "But" confronts the actor. Through this, as through all weather of the seasons, round the will's way must wend.

> The winds whipped in his face, but he marched steadily on.

> The winter had come, but all the animals of the field and forest were snug in their nests under the cover of the white blanket of snow.

"Here Phaethon lies who drove the Sun-god's car. Greatly he failed, but he had greatly dared."

—Ovid

All deeds, actions, verb movements meet with Condition, the "but." But beyond condition there is the rhythmic stride of life, the victory of the Will over all resistance—"When in eternal lines to time thou growst." Shakespeare, who puts this last in his sonnet, speaks out this eternal sense of "and" in a parody form at the end of *Macbeth*:

"Tomorrow and tomorrow and tomorrow creeps in this petty pace from day to day and all our Yesterdays have lighted fools the way to dusty death."

This threefold determination behind the human will, that in its every action:

a) decides,

b) meets consequent conditions, negative and positive,

c) succeeds, and strides eternally on

is the "rationale" behind the three major conjunctions:

Or

But

And

at the basis of all language, which in their conjoining of sentences, mirror this threefold movement of the human soul. From here they are applied to all objects, and used derivatively to connect clauses, phrases, and words as well.

The Subordinate Conjunction conjoins a main sentence with a clause. What this means is that it connects the sentence movement or step of the will with thought. It subordinates the will movement of verb action to the thinking consciousness. The subordinate clause expresses the thought according to which the will, or verb action generally, orders itself when acting. Hence, it links the will life to consciousness. The Subordinate Conjunction thus mediates the connection between will and thought, the verb action in a sentence with its subordinate clause. The Main Conjunction, on the other hand, mediates the pure movement of the will itself in moving from sentence to sentence, without reference to thinking consciousness or rational ground. When not expressed "simply" in simple sentences, but rather in its connection to thought, or "complexly" in complex sentences, the will moves (the verb acts) through the rational screen or by means of the "rationale" of these twelve subordinating-conjunctive forms:

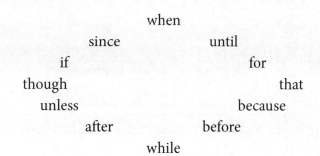

when

since   until

if   for

though   that

unless   because

after   before

while

All other subordinate conjunctions are aspects of these twelve, built up from them, as when the adverb "so" or prepositional unit "in order" is placed before "that," giving "so that," "in order that," or when the adverb "ever" is added to "when" making "whenever," or "even" is put ahead of "though" and "if" combining thus to "even though" and "even if"; or when "all" is prefixed to "though" for "although."

This twelvefold rationale of the conscious human will life indirectly applicable to all verb action, has a very definite wisdom and contains all that fundamentally belongs to the character and concept of action as such. For every event, act, or experience happens at a moment in time ("when"), which has a "before" and an "after"; every event is in a definite period, epoch, or lifetime, connected with others ("while") and in that period has come from a beginning point ("since") and will continue to an end ("until"); every event has a cause ("because"), a reason ("for"), and a purpose ("that"); and every event takes place through what is granted as a positive condition ("if"), or fails to take place in the negative condition ("unless"), and proceeds through contrary condition or resistance ("though").

This twelvefold conception of verb action can therefore be arranged thusly:

Before
When
After

If   Because
Though   For
Unless   That

Since
While
Until

It should be quite obvious even to the untutored eye that we have here to do with a definite intelligent order through which the verb's action (will) moves when its qualifying condition(s) is explicitly stated, i.e. when a Subordinate Clause expressing the connection of the main action to the thought qualifying it is added to the main sentence.

There are four aspects to this matrix of intelligence, each expressed through three definite conjunctions, as illustrated above.

The first aspect is one of outer or "objective determination," governed by the conjunctions "because," "for," and "that." These conjunctions express respectively: cause, reason, and purpose. Now every action is done out of cause, for a reason, and to a purpose, and these are derived from God, Nature, or Man. They are consequently "objectively determinative" of verb action.

Objective Determination
because
for
that

Then there is the aspect of inner, subjective or self determination, which reaches its fullest significance in human action. A human act, or any other, ultimately confronts the positive and negative, or the forces of good and evil, in being executed. That means it can occur or it can not. We express the positive condition by saying the action occurs "if." We express the negative when we say it occurs "unless," i.e. it fails to occur when the negative condition prevails. ("If" and "unless" can work interchangeably as both positive or negative). In addition, all action occurs through a medium of friction with other objects, of resistance of nature, and of tests given by gods and man. Through these, every acting agent must advance, and they are expressed through the "though" (although).

Subjective Determination

if

unless

though

A third aspect comes through the Duration in which an action occurs, or the "while." This duration is a period, epoch, lifetime, wherein actions take place contemporaneously. It extends backward to a definite point or beginning, expressed by "since," and forward "until" a definite point or end.

Duration

while

since

until

Finally there is the aspect of temporal immediacy in all verb action. An action takes place at a definite, perceived point a "when," between a "before," which is remembered and an "after" foreseen.

Immediacy

when

before

after

When this fourfold subordinating principle is applied to man's action as such, it directly points to the four essential aspects of human nature.

Physical Body— (Sense Existence)	determined objectively by cause, reason, purpose, at level of God-Nature
Life Duration—	dwelling in the passing of the body's life from birth to death (since, while, until)
Soul Immediacy—	perceiving the constant conditioning of the moment between remembering and foreseeing (before, when, after)
Self—	determining the act (deed, experience) through-controlled will (if, though, unless)

Where does action, human or other, take place? Action always takes place somewhere, even if "in mind." Hence the vessel or playground for an action, the place of its coming to be, the "where," constitutes one of our Subordinate Conjunctions. Indeed, it underlies them, as a deeper subordination, as it were. Still another, most central conjunction, must be mentioned.

This is the conjunction that signifies how one action runs parallel to another action; not that one action occurs when another occurs, for that is then abrupt, like two units, the one occurring, the other occurring: when A occurs, then B occurs. These two meet, as it were, in the circumstance in which they both occur.

With this other conjunction the case is different. It signifies "equality" to one action occurring by another, a running parallel to it. The Anglo-Saxon word whence this conjunction is derived is "*eal swa*," meaning, literally, "all so" or quite so. The same origin makes the word "also" of course.

The meaning of this conjunction, then, enables the human mind to conceive of an act, event, or experience happening "here" (that is, some "where") and standing or being in an "equal" moving place with another act that occurs all so i.e. same in every way and manner. As, for example, dying out of earth life and awakening to the life of the heavens: or dying out of the heavens and being born into earth life. Two actions, though entirely separate as actions, from seemingly different places (one here one there, one somewhere the other elsewhere). Yet "all so" or "equal" to one another in the event of occurring the one "coming out" of the one same source, in principle, as the other.

Such a word exists in the language! And in a curious way, being a most common word, it points, when it is exactly understood, to something opposite in meaning to the "where," which we conceive of outwardly, as a place, or a containing. It points, namely, to some intelligence or inward source (of being) that permits, in the nature of things, the exact synchronization of two events happening in the world at once. And this little word is: "As."

As the last rays of the sun were fading, a rose hue on the horizon, the twilight glance of Venus, first star of the evening, was softly radiating out of the still lightened fleece of blue in the sky, following, a love's echo, in its wake.

We have then, the Round Table of Twelve Subordinate Conjunctions arranged in related groups of three each, all grounded with a middle, which has an outward side—the "where"—and an inward side—the "as"—through which the latter and only therethrough (for "when" or "while" can't cover such instance) the "eventing" (e =venire= coming out) or occurring of two or more actions in the same way is possible. Every man walks with these twelve,acts, thinks, speaks through them or in their qualifying presence, and so far as he has a body he is the outer side or "where" he acts, and so far that he is a soul, he has an inner side which acts in simultaneity with, at the same time as, or "as" the body acts. The Body—through the eye—sees into the world, and the Spirit—through the I—thinks through what the eye beholds, but it is the Soul which forms the meeting ground within, so that man can accomplish and be conscious of the fact: as the body perceives, the mind comprehends; as I am seeing, I am simultaneously conceiving.

Because

For

That

Since	Where	Before
While	As	When
Until		After

If

Though

Unless

This is Subordination of Action (will) to Mind (thought or Reason), with respect to an objective determining (*God-Nature*), a sphere of duration and immediacy connected with all (action) that lives and senses (*Soul*), and a subjective determining or being confronted with positive and negative poles in a natural medium of resistance—our experiential sphere or *World*. Now the English Tongue treats the whole sphere of Verb Action through the compass of this Shield of Subordination which it holds up in front of itself, protecting, receiving blows of undirected qualifying action, as with the mighty sentence stroke it wields the sword of speech, proclaiming its advance.

The basic ingredients of all exclamations are the vowels, which in their pure form, as immediate inner response to outer impression, are themselves interjections:

Ah

a

ee

oh

oo

Consider: God! Hey! Yippee! Holy cow! Oo la la!
Interjections can be phrases

"Land sakes alive!

Over my dead body!

Heavens to Betsy!

Jumping Jehosophet!

By Saint George!

Or whole sentences:

Well, I'll be hog swoggled!

Would you believe it!

Are you serious!

What hath God wrought!

—Samuel F. B. Morse, First dispatch by telegraph, 1840

Some typical and colorful exclamations are:

Really!	Brother!
No Kidding!	Fabulous!
Yeah!	Fantastic!
Gee whiz!	Nonsense!
Golly!	Swell!
Gosh!	Good gravy! (Good gracious!)
Jolly Good!	Lawdy, lawdy!
Smashing!	I'll tell the world!
Wow!	Zounds!
Bah! (Humbug!)	Great day in the morning!
Son of a Gun!	Ain't that somethin'!
Jeepers!	Boy o'boy!
Honest to Goodness!	That's the last straw!

That's a lot of hooey!

Never in a thousand years!

Hosannah!

Hallelujah!

Hotdog!

For the love of Pete!

Terrific!

Great!

Beautiful!

The interjection or exclamation in its less emphatic form does not separate from the sentence:

"But, soft! What light through yonder window breaks? It is the east, and Juliet is the sun!"

"O Romeo, Romeo! Wherefore art thou Romeo?"

"Oh, praised be the beauty of this earth: the beauty, and the bloom, and the mirthfulness thereof!"

—Melville

Interjection means "to throw between." Between me and the world, between the subject and the object, an expression, reaction or response is thrown. The inner life is sounded forth in feeling. The true Poet is he, who seeing wisdom in the world and uniting with it in thought, holds up his pure heart like a lyre, thereto and records the tones of unadulterated response called forth by a wisdom-conceived world in a form whose very content, rhythm, and meaning is the "higher feeling," or "nobler interjection" of a transformed human nature.

PRONOUN

The idea of the Pronoun is threefold: that which precedes the noun (or name state), that which proceeds from the noun, or that which substitutes for the noun. These three aspects are already given through the prefix "pro," which means: before, or for (in place of), or forth, onward. Therefore the word pronoun means, literally:

a) before the noun

b) in place of the noun

Personal: I, we, you, you, he, she, it, they

Indefinite:

all / none	former / latter
everything / nothing	everyone / no one
each / every	everybody / nobody
same / other	some / something
one / many	any / anything
few / much	someone / somebody
either / neither	anyone / anybody
ought / naught	each other / one another
both / such	several / another
certain / sundry	

Relative: who

which

that

Intensive: myself, ourselves, yourself, yourselves, himself, herself, itself, themselves

Reflexive: same as Intensive

The being of the Pronoun is a book of seven seals, it mirrors the mystery of the arising of human consciousness and the originating of the polarity: I and the world. It represents in its three-fold function the movement the human consciousness goes through from:

1) its pre-thinking, pre-Noun state, where it lives immediately connected by mere perception to the activities of the world before registering and ordering these as noun forms, to

2) the thinking state wherein it names (or "nouns") the activities of the world, bringing them into the recognized pictorial form of our surrounding sense world, to

3) the post noun state of after-image inwardized consciousness, wherein the cognized percepts or named objects (nouns) of the world live on in the soul as the store of memory, a possession constituting an inner self-consciousness over against the immediate sense awareness of the world.

Consider such sentences as:

It is raining.

It is snowing.

It is getting late.

They refer to activities through the pronoun. These verb activities are not centered in a definite named subject. They are pre-noun affirmations, before the world has been put under label and capped with name. They are "throw backs" in the language, remnants of yore, when human consciousness lived less intellectually with the world, closer to the Word in its omnipresent action of all things. In principle all sentences expressing the Noun State (our ordinary state of consciousness) predicate verb action of a definite noun, such as:

The sun is shining.

Nature is burgeoning.

Mankind is ripening.

In the German language, by its use of the Dative Case, which is one of its chief characteristics, the action of the subject can still in certain cases be expressed as coming from the pronoun:

Es ist mir gelungen.   (I succeeded, literally: It is to me succeeded.)

a sorry, li   It does to me sorrow.)

a afrad, li   y: It horrors to me.)

 it histor   reference to human consciousness, ex-
 the act   activities of the beings of the world we
 moy p   onstituting our own innr life. The verb
 n of the   subject. This is mirrored grammatically

The shining sun.

Thus we have a linguistic movement grammatically which we can classify as a movement from the

This movement is the tonic chord in all language, the very reason or justification of its being, because it mirrors linguistically the nature of human consciousness: how it evolves and how it operates.

Using this trichotomy as basic outline, let us trace the progressive movement through the seven forms of the Pronoun in the order given above to the proper duality "I and the World." Normally, in the everyday state of mind, pronouns substitute for nouns. Where I would say John or Mary, I say he or she; where I would otherwise have to iterate names of persons or objects, I can economize with all, some, both, none (of them), etc.; where I would need to give the designations of objects, I say simple this and that; and by using which or who or that I can enumerate a variety of predications of a subject without every time repeating the Noun.

Consciousness in its simplest state is "demonstrative":

What's that over there? (Why, that's the entrance to a secret cave.)

Look at these! (They're violets already in bloom.)

That's late! (About the arrival time of a train.)

0 this is great fun! (On a roller coaster.)

I think I'll take that one. (Picking out a melon at the grocer's.)

"This above all, to thine own self be true."
—Shakespeare

We demonstrate by pointing with the finger or gesturing with arm and hand, explicitly or in a mental gesture. A child uses the demonstrative pronoun first before she can speak the names of the objects around her, for the human being moves her limbs before she thinks. The first pronominal duality leading to the main polarity "I and the World" is the demonstrative duality:

This — That

expressing in terms of mere presence, near and far, man's sense of space and time, the here—there and now—then at the root of a consciousness of "World."

Long before the inner reference to a center of consciousness ("I") has been personally named, or its corresponding outer reference ("It") elaborated as noun, human consciousness can refer "indefinitely" to itself and the things and beings around it as: all, some, several, each, one, et.al.

To each his own.

Many are called, few are chosen.

All was made through the Word, and none of the made was made, but through the Word.
—St. John

"Something there is in the float of the sight of things that provokes it out of the soul."
—Walt Whitman

"I become a transparent eyeball; I am nothing; I see all; the currents of the Universal Being circulate through me; I am part or parcel of God."
—Ralph Waldo Emerson

With these pronouns we comprehend the objects of the world not yet in definite name (nouns), but through an indefinite mathematical"more or less." We throw, as it were, a loose net over the things of the world and pull them in by ones, or pairs, or groups, or as a whole, or the former or latter, some first, others last, the same and the different, and such as they all are.

These indefinite pronouns, when not standing directly for the unnamed objects or nouns, refer indirectly to a definite whole through the Genitive:

> Not one of the candles in the great hall was burning, none of the servants were about, all of the rooms were dark and still, some of the neighborhood owls were heard hooting, as we passed, both of us clinging closely together, neither of us daring to breathe, down the narrow passageway, which led to the deep moat at the bottom of the wall, near whose edge a few of the boats were moored, ready for the possible use of any of those braver and stronger souls (few of which were yet alive) in their attempt to escape the evils of this renowned castle, of whose prisoners many had reached the outer air of freedom.

The most characteristic duality in this "Net of Comprehension" of the Indefinite Pronouns is that of:

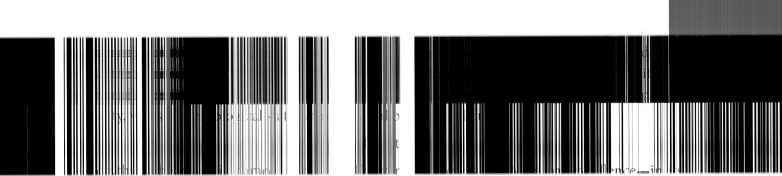

I and It.

This "It" opposed to the I, if a person, singular or plural, directly spoken to (for the personal pronouns are determined by the quality and manner of the speaking ego) is "You." If it is a person (or persons) indirectly spoken of it is "he," "she," or "they." And if the I considers plurality from its own standpoint, it speaks "we."

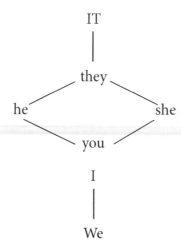

This eightfold dynamic act of "person" in Pronoun Consciousness is the first mode of the soul's orientation among men on earth. Every human agent contains it as the unspun web-silk of interrelationship spun like the spider spins his web, not in the light of the sun, but in the light raying from the human heart, in accordance with which it then, at will, operates socially in the world.

Only with respect to the Personal Pronouns does the English Language still have cases:

Nominative	Possessive	Objective
I	Mine	Me
We	Ours	Us
You	Yours	You
You	Yours	You
It	Its	It
He	His	Him
She	Hers	Her
They	Theirs	Them

Who, referring to persons is also declined:

Who	Whose	Whom

The Possessive case is "genitive," the Objective case is both "dative" and "accusative," which in English are the same.

He knew them.   He went with them.

With the emergence of the "I-It" duality in the progressive development of human consciousness, there arise two additional ways in which man begins to consciously reflect upon his own person—either upon himself as object (Reflexive Pronoun):

or stituting a duality—the su-
sons and objects) awakens o
lself in the round, so to speak,
rg back or in upon oneself s
ive) aspect thereof, creates the
ogation in which the question

the world, to its inner meaning and the meaning of the earth, names it and names himself, raises his consciousness from the merely impersonal, undefined, undifferentiated Pronoun State, to the state of Noun or Name Consciousness.

Of these seven Interrogative Pronouns, Who and Which are relative pronouns not primary as question form but presupposing for their interrogative function an object already qualified as noun. Hence we have basically to do with a Fivefold Form of Interrogation, the Five Pointed Star:

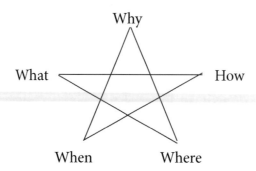

In this fivefold interrogative perspective, man looks out into the world and asks:

What is it?   — This is the question about Substance — the root question of all Science.

How is it?   — This is the question about technique or Method and Mode of Creation — the root question of all Art.

Why is it?   —This is the question of Cause— the root question of all Religion.

When is it?   — This is the question about Place and Time — the questions rooted in the Planetary Consciousness of the Earth.

In carving these lead lines of interrogation as Stellar—Quest into consciousness, the soul of man orientates itself in the world and orders from within outward around itself a "universe." In our larger grammar we may treat of these things in more detail; here let us simply indicate. The echo answering to the question form is first, simply, this same form reversed, becoming therewith a statement, e.g.:

It is what (it is).

Thus the fundamental duality in the Interrogative Pronoun Consciousness is the question form and its reversal into answer form:

What is it? — It is what.

Now this state of answer, retaining, as it does, the interrogative Pronoun and acquiring a clause form (having subject and verb) is in form though not yet in content, a Noun. For in asking e.g. "What is it?" and answering, say,

It is the sky.

But in its more mature, properly definitive form, in better language as such, there rises out of this Answer Form, the Noun Clause.

Write a series of sentences with such clauses using all the pronouns with regular verbs, such as:

When the clock strikes eight…

Where the ships go out to sea…

How the pearl comes to be…

Why there is evil…

Etc.

RELATIVE

Now what happens in human consciousness when the step is made to the Relative Clause? This is the spot in which human consciousness "goes full circle." That which is first in front of us as perception comes through us from behind as the subjective act of our mind, and the conception of the perceived (object) receives "dropwise" from its circling Idea the predications (concepts) belonging to it.

The tree —which is standing by the river bank

which is a Willow

whose branches reach down to the water's edge

which sways and rustles in the wind

under which the maiden sits

dreaming of her love

from whose branch the shepherd

boy whittles a rustic flute

round whose trunk the children

dance and sing,

which is hoary with age and

mighty in breadth

in whose branches the birds

sit chirping in their nest

the shade of which is balsam

on hot summer days

which lies on the rivers bend just

where the fishing is best.

The predications given through the Relative Clause are manifold and infinite respecting the objects of this world, infinite respecting God and the All.

"Our Father Who art in the heavens" _____ is,

according to the point of view herein represented, a path of cognition stretching infinitely before us.

Note: The word "that," one of the most common in the language, is, as connective pronoun, to be understood as related to the interrogative What and derived from it as follows:

What do you know?
I know that he will come.

What is a wonder?
It is a wonder that she is still living.

As Relative Pronoun proper it is used instead of the world "what." Given:

What do I see — I see a tree

and using the answer form of the clause to modify the object seen i.e. as Relative Clause, we do not say:

The tree what I see is an Oak

but

The tree that (or which) I see is an Oak.

With the other Interrogative Pronouns this is not the case, e.g.:

Where do I bathe — I bathe at the beach.

The beach where I bathe is sandy.

We have been considering the Pronoun in an evolutionary sense, as a movement from Pre-Noun to the Noun form and then to the Post-Noun form, wherein is brought to expression how human consciousness, attaining increasingly higher states through seven distinct stages, progressively awakens to the Self. These stages are:

The Duality of Demonstration—	This—That —	At the level of Place or bodily presence
The Duality of Indefiniteness—	All—None— One—Many	At the level of increase and decrease in a mathematical range
The Duality of Person—	I—It	At the level of division into Personal Gender
The Duality of Intention and	Myself—Itself	At the level of rational Reflection movement into subject and object
The Duality of Interrogation—	What is it—It is What	At the level of precognitive thought
The Duality of Relation—	That—Which	At the level of thinking cognition

72

Thus through the pronoun as adjective, the noun, in addition to being conceived, is concretized, centered or individualized into the mind.

Now the Noun through the sixfold generation of the Pronoun (regarding Intensive and Reflexive as a unity) experiences or enacts a differentiation equivalent to what the Verb experiences in the sixfold generation of its tenses, and there is a direct correspondence between the Verb and its six tenses and the Noun and its six pronouns. Further, as we have seen, the Noun, respecting its signification, has in the pronouns a prior, a present, and a posterior. So the Verb has a past, a present, and a future.

Thus the great temporal movement of Before–Now–After met with in the action of the verb as Present–Past–Future is present in the nature of the pronoun in respect to its relation to the Noun. As a verb goes through past, present, and future in time, the pronoun, in its collective being, goes from Pre-Noun through Noun to Post-Noun in the movement of its signification. Hence there is a parallel between the role of the noun in its relation to the verb and in its relation to the pronoun. It is in both cases the "subject" round which their activity and signification centers.

The noun is the proper subject of the verb's action; it is likewise the subject of the pronoun's signification. The pronoun foreshadows the noun; the verb proceeds from it as an act.

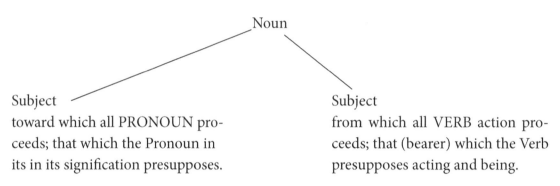

Noun

Subject
toward which all PRONOUN proceeds; that which the Pronoun in its in its signification presupposes.

Subject
from which all VERB action proceeds; that (bearer) which the Verb presupposes acting and being.

THE OCTAVE

We are now at the point of being able, in the review of this chapter, to observe the Octave Movement in the language: the movement from the Pronoun Form of Sentence Consciousness to the Noun Form of Sentence Consciousness, or, quite simply: from the Pronoun Sentence, which is tonic and the first, to the Noun Sentence, being the octave thereof. Take as example the sentence:

It is clearing up.

The truth, herewith expressed, is a perception made "in general" at the point of a perfect immediacy without all modification. The perception is absolute—a deeper point in balance between Subject and Verb.

Now, as soon as a noun is substituted for the pronoun and a "specification" thereby effected, all noun modification begins.

Interjection

Pronoun   Verb

Noun   SENTENCE   Verb

Adjective   Adverb

Preposition

Conjunction

Preposition

Adverb   Adjective

Verb   SENTENCE   Noun

Verb   Pronoun

Interjection

is nonsense unless it is indicative: You shall go, You did go. The Imperative expresses the point of view of the Body. It is the consciousness of being fully incarnate in the Present and in absolute confrontation and interaction with the world. It is body—determined, literally the voice of the body and limbs:

> Hand me that flashlight.
>
> Answer the phone.
>
> Go out and get the mail.
>
> Tie your shoes.
>
> Comb your hair.
>
> Buy me an ice cream cone.
>
> Take the evening plane.
>
> Tuck in your shirt.

And when the soul or spirit is addressed instead of the body, it is done so in the mood of concrete bodily immediacy:

> Don't put on airs!
>
> Get your mind out of the gutter!
>
> Have a heart!
>
> Think!
>
> "Make straight the ways of the Lord!"
> —St. John
>
> "Be ye therefore perfect as your Father is perfect..."
> —St. Paul

Make a list of at least fifty of the most common everyday imperatives used in English, as, for Example: open the window, answer the phone, pass the pepper, be quiet, wake up, come on, etc. Then write a proper series of command form sentences describing the situation in which they occur.

INDICATIVE

The Indicative Mood covers all the normal verb tenses in both active and passive voice, simple and continuous form, question and negation.

Indicative

Present				Future
Past				Perfect
Future			Past	
	Present		Perfect	
	Perfect			

unrealized "higher self," out of which he gazes forward and plans how it shall be, sets his sights on higher, newer aims, sets goals for this progress and ennoblement. In its fully realized state it is the state of so-called "paradise," the perfection of human nature, or angel consciousness. Insofar as the angel works from the next higher plane of development into our soul nature, we have the Subjunctive mood. It is the working into the human of the angelic consciousness.

The scale of mood in the Subjunctive runs from the trivial to the profound with all degrees in-between. Consider the end of Romeo's soliloquy about Juliet whom he sees on the balcony:

> "See! how she leans her cheek upon her hand:
> O! that I were a glove upon that hand
> That I might touch that cheek."
> —William Shakespeare, Romeo and Juliet

Consider Hamlet in his second soliloquy bewailing his own indecision after witnessing the players he hires to sound the king's conscience:

> "Is it not monstrous that this player here,
> Could force his soul so to his own conceit
> That from her working all his visage wann'd...
> What's Hecuba to him or he to Hecuba
> That he should weep for her?
> What would he do
> Had he the motive and the cue for passion
> That I have?
> He would drown the stage with tears,
> And cleave the general ear with horrid speech.
> Make mad the guilty and appall the free,
> Confound the ignorant, and amaze indeed
> The very faculties of eyes and ears."
> —Shakespeare, Hamlet

Or Lady Macbeth calling down her insidious inspiration:

> "Come, thick night,
> And pall thee in the dunnest smoke of hell,
> That my keen knife see not the wound it makes,
> Nor heaven peep through the blanket of the dark,
> To cry 'Hold, hold!'"

(Here the "s" is dropped in the third person singular to create Subjunctive Mood.)

Consider Benjamin Franklin in a letter to a friend about his newly invented "Lightening Rod":

> "...may not the knowledge of this power of points be of use to mankind, in preserving houses, churches, ships, etc., from the stroke of lightening by...Would not these pointed

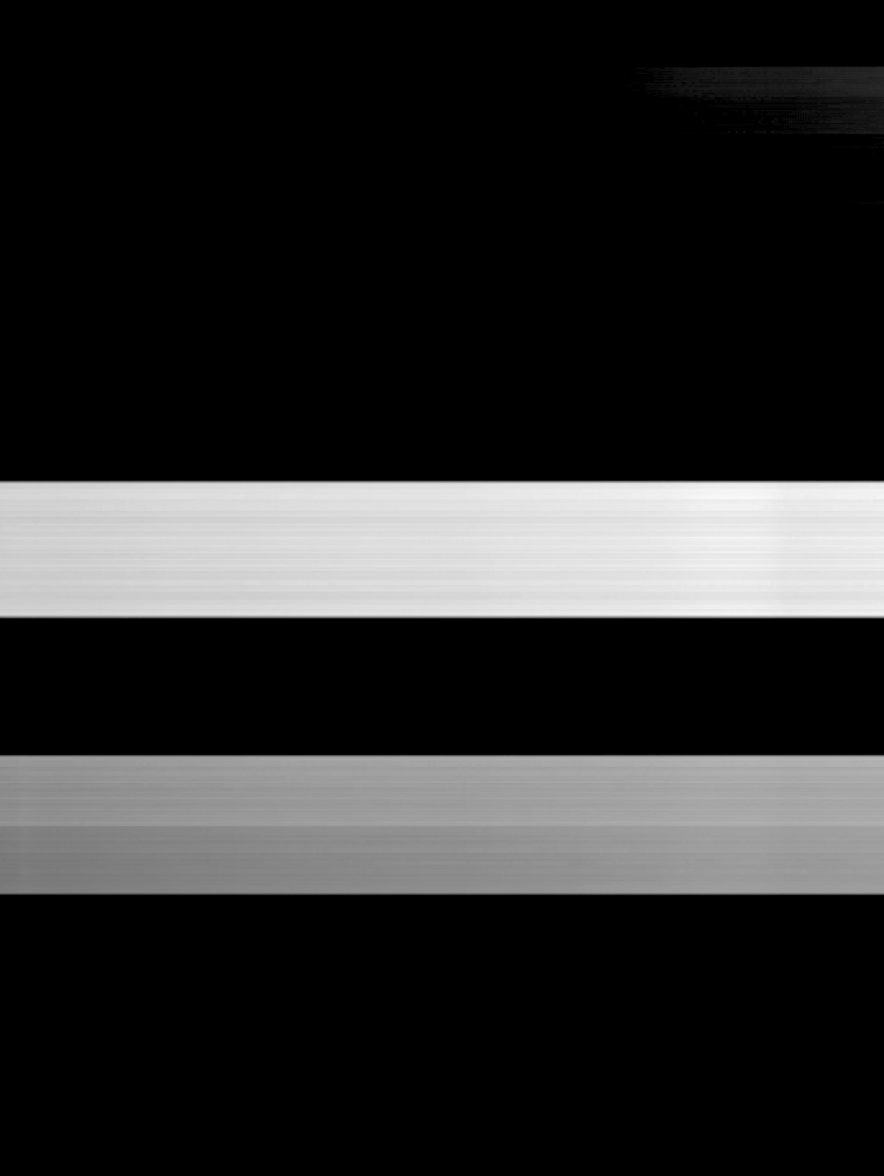

gentle rain, binding heaven closer to the earth, tis then an inner cheer that fills the soul with warmth, and calls up that cozy mood we feel of natural romance.

Put the following text into Indicative Mood:

> Were he to come then would I be certain. Not as now would I be tossed in turmoil and travail, be tempted into thousand moods of mischief, nor should I suffer the abominations of remorse my mind would constantly be throwing up against itself. If but a word, an echo of a word should reach my hungry heart, should I be then so tumultuously unsure, should I be so alone! Aye, he were truly as a God who now should appear. And with all my heart I would that he would come.

The Subjunctive defines an event that might happen or may happen, that could happen that can or is able to happen, that should or ought to happen or perhaps shall, that must or has to happen, that wants to or would like to happen, but does not define an event that is happening, did happen or has happened, had happened, will happen or will have happened. In other words it is not in the clear day of indicative time, but in the cloudy, stormy uncertain weather of unrealized will. The connection between the will of the subject acting and the act or event to take place has not yet been consummated. We say:

He must	—Necessity
He has to	
He can	—Capacity (ability)
He is able to	
He may	— Lawfulness
He is allowed to Allowance (permission)	
He should	—Duty, Rightfulnes^s
He ought (to)	
He wants to	— Desire
He would like (to) —Wish	

Through these five spheres of soul mood the subject goes before the will consummates in an act. These are the assisting, preparatory stages, hence are called "auxiliary verbs" or "modal auxiliaries" for they define the inner soul attitude preceding action and event. Once so prepared, we can say:

He might	—Possibility
He may	

Thus we see, in these modal auxiliaries, a sixfold sense toward every act, toward acting, as such, built into every human being. His physical body gives him the capacity; life in him and its

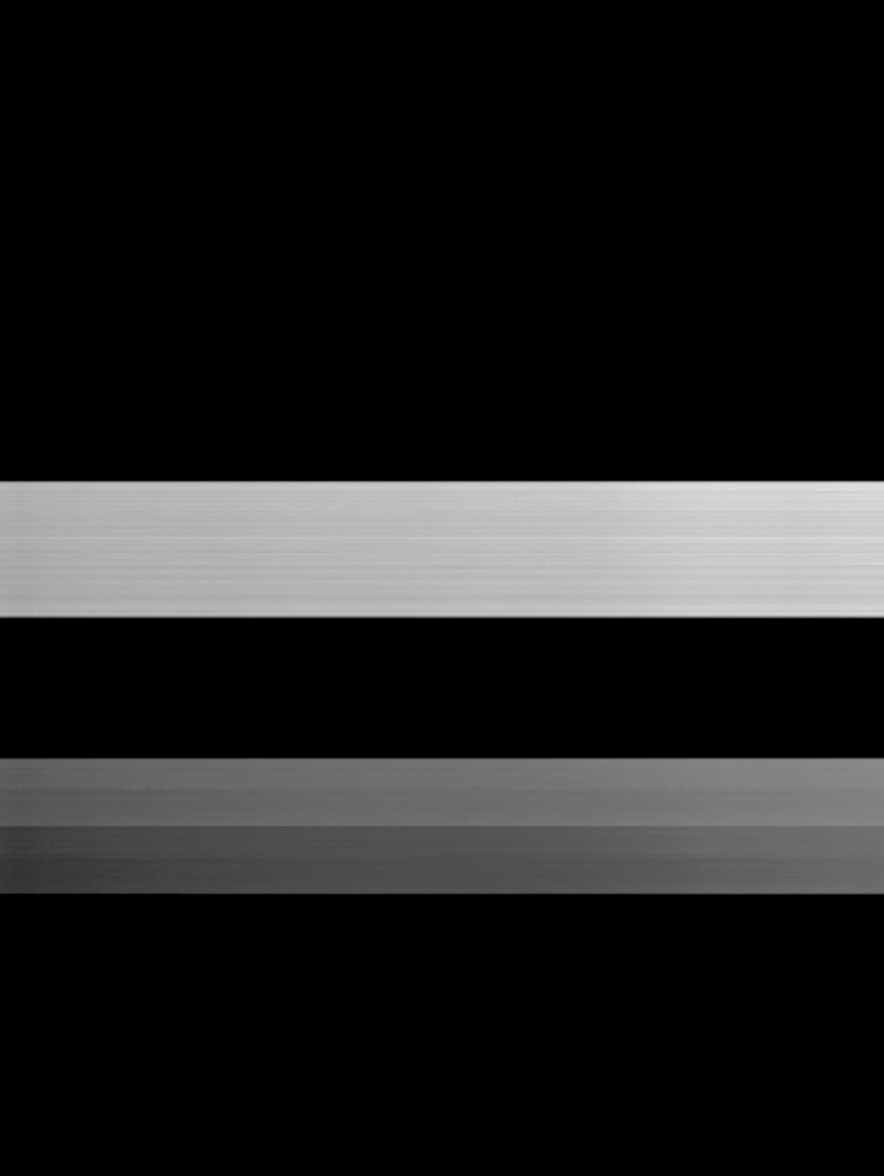

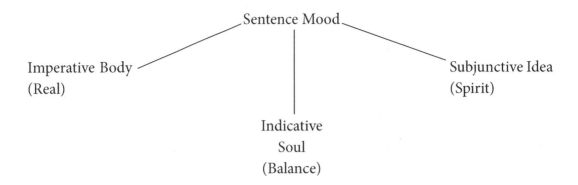

In the Imperative the Will is too far Forward, too intense in the Real; in the Subjunctive the Will is unborn, too far backward, still in the Ideal; in the Indicative the Will lives naturally in the balance between inner and outer, idea and reality, in its own proper element.

Note: Apart from the

> I shall (act) — indicative auxiliary
> I would (act)— subjunctive condition
> I want (to)— subjunctive wish
> I would like (to)

the English language has the verb "to will," which expresses purely in a direct sense the Will:

> I will the deed.
> I will to do it.
> I will peace.

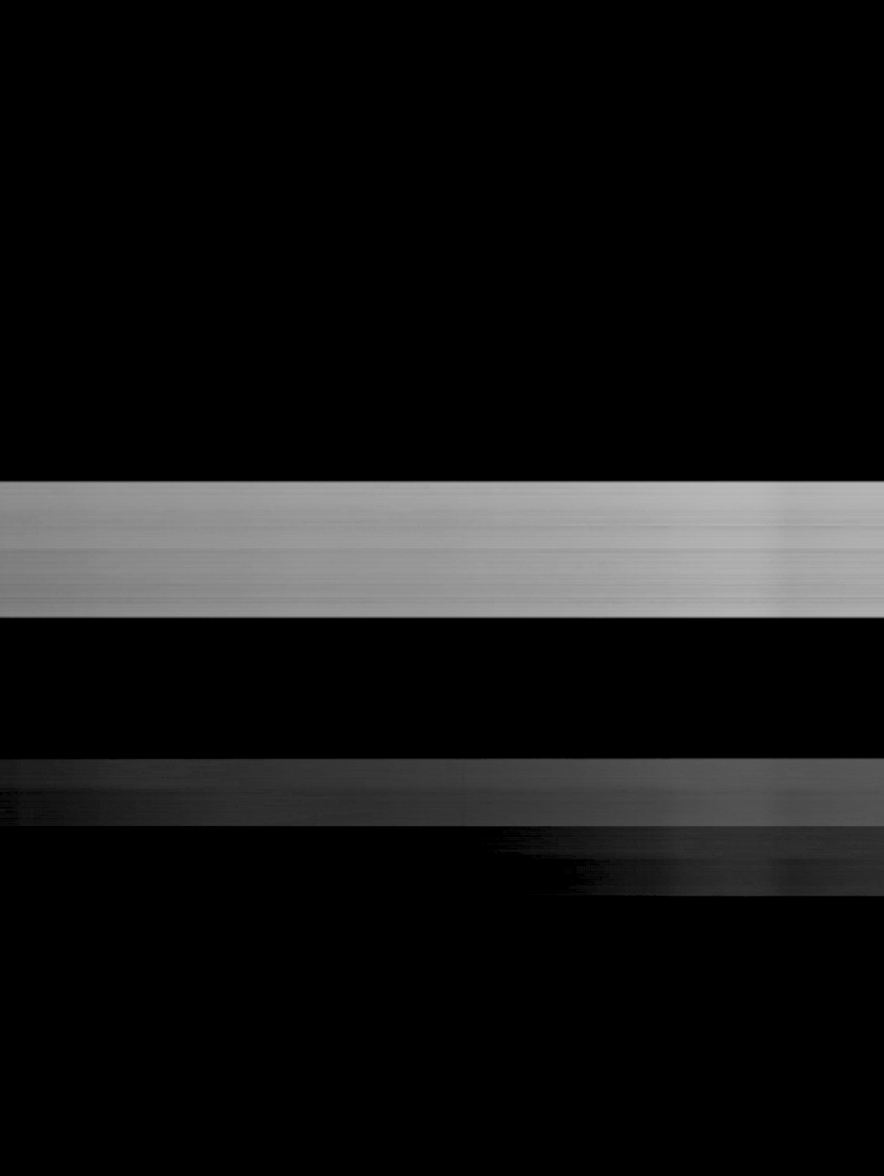

A compound sentence is a combination or conjoining of two or more simple sentences.

> Roses are flowering in the garden and love is flowering in her heart.

> "Either all things proceed from one intelligent source and come together as in one body, and the part ought not to find fault with what is done for the benefit of the whole; or there are only atoms, and nothing else than mixture and dispersion."
>
> —Marcus Aurelius

A complex sentence is a conjoining of a main clause with one or more subordinate clauses in a sentence, i.e. a simple sentence with one or more dependent clauses.

> "Once upon a time there was a King who had three sons, two of which were clever and smart, but the third was naive and simple, and was called Sillybones."
>
> —Grimm's Fairy Tales

> "And when they settled down, there they lay in just the very position the Snow Queen had told Kay he must find out, if he was to become his own master and have the whole world and a new pair of skates."
>
> —Hans Christian Anderson, "The Snow Queen"

> "If it be the sacred province and— by the wisest, deemed— the inestimable compensation of the heavier woes, that they both purge the soul of gay—hearted errors and replenish it with a saddened truth; that holy office is not so much accomplished by any covertly inductive reasoning process, whose original motive is received from the particular affliction; as it is the magical effect of the admission into man's inmost spirit of a before inexperienced and wholly inexplicable element, which like electricity suddenly received into any sultry atmosphere of the dark, in all directions splits itself into nimble lances of purifying light; which at one and the same instant discharge all the air of sluggishness and inform it with an illuminating property; so that objects which before, in the uncertainty of the dark, assumed shadowy and romantic outlines, now are lighted up in their substantial realities; so that in these flashing revelations of grief's wonderful fire, we see all things as they are; and though when the electric element is gone, the shadows once more descend, and the false outlines of objects again return; yet not with their former power to deceive; for now, even in the presence of the falsest aspects, we still retain impressions of their immovable true ones, though indeed, once more concealed."
>
> —Melville, *Pierre*

There are basically these three types of sentence: Simple, Compound, and Complex. The Submerged Sentence is actually the Complex Sentence "re-simplified." Being done consciously and with cognition, however, it involves the whole art of sentence style which this chapter sets forth to propound.

SIMPLE

The simple sentence is used to express action: it is effective, compact, and has the quality of defining. There is also something fresh and invigorating, immediate and dramatic about the simple

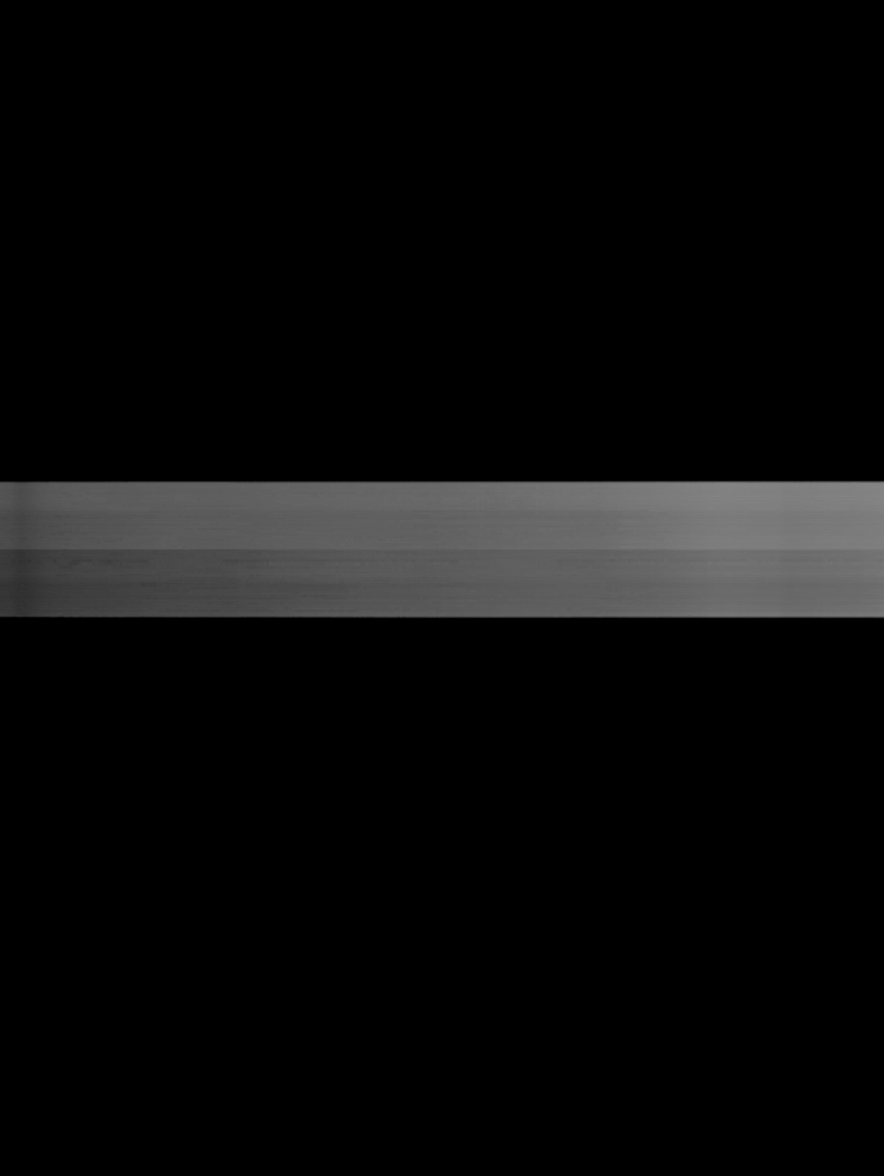

The simple sentence is also used as the practical language of the limbs:

> Take the Corn Flakes box with the left hand. Hold it on the top close to the middle between the thumb and the remaining fingers. Fasten your attention on the perforated line near the top of the right side. You will read "punch in here." Do so with the right thumb, nail facing downwards. Press the flap inward up against the roof of the package. Now rip slowly upward to reveal the inner plastic bag. Take this bag by its corner firmly be tween your teeth and tear it open by a jerky sideways movement of the head. Spit out the bitten-off corner of the plastic bag. Now take hold of the inner plastic bag and with the thumbs rip it wider open. The opening should be wide enough to allow a generous portion of the contents to fall rustling into a bowl. Fetch said bowl. Then grasp the box in the right hand and pour. Add milk and sugar according to taste. Fresh fruit, such as peaches or berries (in season) are to be recommended. Now sit down and enjoy yourself. For full satisfaction we suggest two bowls.

COMPOUND

The Compound Sentence is used to row and rank things together, to connect them in such a way as to produce a successive rhythmical movement, ascending, descending like the waves of the sea, flowing on like a river:

> He joined the circle, but he retained his own individual character. He used their language, but he spoke his thoughts. He fought in their battles, but the accents of his movements belonged to himself. He was bound by the outer custom and manner, but inwardly he was free.

> They gathered their forces together and marched to the field, and there they met the foe, and they fought and they fought and they fought, for hour on hour, till they could fight no more; and then they sent their second strength in quickness everywhere into that field, and they struck blow on blow; they lashed and lanced and leveled and fought and they wrought the victory and took the day—and day for day from then till now this gallant band has held that field and built in power the founding form of truth.

This rhythmic building form of sentence movement through the Compound Sentence cannot be created either by the crystalline earth staccato of the sentence simple in its radial force quality, or the interweaving, broader sweeping, petal forming quality of the Complex Sentence. It is rather the movement of water in all its manifold forms that the Sentence Compound brings, transformed, to life in human speech.

COMPLEX

In the Complex Sentence we are in a yet more subtle movement than that of the crystal earth element of the Simple Sentence or of the rhythmic water element of the Compound Sentence. The Complex sentence, as we have seen, branches out in three ways from the main sentence trunk as Relative, Subordinate, and Noun Clause. These three dependent clause movements give possibility of endless variation and pave the way for a thoroughly differentiated use of the fantasy.

Although the street, which seemed like a melting pot for all peoples, tribes and races, was crowded to a degree unknown before, making use of the shifting technique of his college football days and an unusually fine directional sense, he wriggled his way through the moving mass, and thus succeeded in attaining a place under the outhanging signs of a row of shops on the far end of the block, where, for some reason, the tension of the market bustle, so like the center of stillness written of a whirlwind, seemed to reduce to a peaceful station, and there with attentive eye to the variegated movements of the masquerading scene before him, he waited for the party he had planned to meet here in this Oriental Bazaar.

Consider the text:

John Baron owns a house in the middle of the city. The house has a large garden. The garden is full of bushes and trees. It is an ideal refuge for migrating birds. Many of them stop here on their way up North.

A.   Above are five simple sentences combined in good style to give a simple description about a house in the city. Now change these five sentences into Compound sentences, retaining the good style of the narrative, but bringing out the characteristic of the Compound Sentence. You will obviously not link them together in a chain—that is no style—but, perhaps, two together, two together, and one alone.

Recall the three "main conjunctions" to be used in making compound sentences: and, but, or. Not all three may fit. If not use the one, or two that do.

B.   After compounding this group of sentences, make Complex sentences of them. Again, do not force all sentences into a chain if it is not good style, but two, perhaps, and then three together. Remember too, that not all of the three types of clauses may work. Choose the right "subordinate conjunction" in making a sentence into a subordinate clause.

Practice the same "reforming" into Compound and Complex Sentences with the following texts:

It is the custom in Rome to pitch a penny in the fountain and make a wish. We followed the custom gallantly. We were a company of 150. Consequently, we covered the whole bottom of the fountain with copper.

Stuttgart is a city in southern Germany. It lies in a valley. The valley is surrounded by lovely hills. The air in the city is often muggy. On the hills it is sweet and clear. The hallmark of Stuttgart was once the "*Stiftskirche*." Now the hallmark is the Television Tower. You can see it already driving in from afar.

The sea gull is a bird. It possesses strong wings. It can fly over large bodies of water. This one can witness. It has the habit of following ships. Often it accompanies them across the whole ocean. The gull maintains its flight by gliding in the currents of the wind. Otherwise it would surely fall exhausted into the sea.

Arthur went to the city. He had a date with a sales representative. He did not know the exact address. The bus brought him to the right street. He had a rule. He always allowed himself enough time. In this way he would avoid coming late. It might happen that he would get held up. In such a case he would call. Today he had plenty of time.

His office, located in the Empire State Building…

His office, in the Empire State Building…

b) The ship which is anchored on the left shore of the harbor…

The ship, anchored on the left shore of the harbor…

The ship, on the left shore of the harbor…

c) The pupil, who was the teacher's favorite…

The pupil, the teacher's favorite…

The teacher's favorite pupil…

This is a way to delete the relative clause. In the last example the phrase is reduced right down to the front position of the adjective, for all relative clauses, as we have before seen, are adjectival.

Reduce the Relative Clauses in the following text to phrases using the above techniques:

On an early mom long ago, a man who was dressed in a wanderer's robe walked up the lane that led to a castle which was situated on a hill that overlooked a wooded vale. What was it which stood next to the entranceway? It was a large oak, which had stood there over 200 years and which had grown to mighty dimensions. On one of the branches there was a shield that hung there and that bore the coat of arms of the owner of the castle, who was a count and who was renowned in that country. The wanderer, who was carrying a staff, struck the shield with it. The sound, which rang like thunder, was carried by the wind down into the valley, through which ran a river. And the country people, who lived in the little village which lay on the riverside, awoke.

Do the same with this text:

The steps, which led to the temple, were broad and steep and made of a white granite which was found near a lake that lay in the southern part of the land. The river which flowed past the quarry was bordered by reeds which swayed gently in the winds that ever blew in those parts. Hot was the sun which constantly shone, and all the birds that lived in the high grass and built their nests in the reeds, all the animals that inhabited the long narrow valley, all life which came into being in that region of the earth, owed its existence to this admirable river, that flowed in timeless tranquillity through the land, that flooded and ebbed with an exact rhythm, a rhythm which took its course from the stars.

Submerging Subordinates:

a) They took the canyon trip, for it was a good opportunity to study the earth strata.

They took the canyon trip, it being a good opportunity to study the earth strata.

They took the canyon trip, a good opportunity to study the earth strata.

and the river full of surprises, they only dressed in bathing suits. If you can imagine a more delightful way to spend a summer's day than that on which you paddle down a crystal river that winds through forests and fields, by farm houses and under bridges and on which you are accompanied by the daring flights and chirping warble of the birds that pervade the river banks when the trees, bushes, and reeds which line them are in midsummer flower, and on which though you swiftly glide with the rapid current down the stream you can, at times, still catch sight of the silver fish resting in the shade under the lily pads, and feel the soft summer breezes while they waft playfully round you—if you can imagine what were more delight than this, then tell it me!

After practicing on this text take the four previous texts used for compounding and subordinating, and "submerge" them in as many ways as an efficient and excelling style leaves open to the fantasy. With smaller texts this can often be done with one excellent sentential movement. One should learn to feel the language in its seven foundational elements—Relative Clause, Subordinate Clause, Noun Clause, Infinitive Phrase, Prepositional Phrase, Present Participial Phrase, and Past participial Phrase—as movement, as seven qualitatively unique movements, different in their "elements" as the seven colors of the rainbow and the seven intervals of the musical scale, distinct from one another in movement as are the seven planets of our solar system.

Let us review our Sentence Movement, considering the "movements" we have learned. Beginning with the Simple Sentence we have the three movements of:

Apposing—	one sentence becomes Apposition of the other:
	The little girl enjoyed her treat. It was a cherry lollipop.
	The little girl enjoyed her treat— a cherry lollipop.
Compounding—	The jets flew in squadron. They peeled off silently.
	The jets flew in squadron, and they peeled off silently.
Rendering Complex—	The squirrels worked furiously gathering their nuts. The winter would soon be upon them.
	The squirrels worked furiously gathering nuts, for the winter would soon be upon them.

We have learned from Chapter II how to "distill" from a sentence the golden essence of the Participial Phrases.

Past Participle Phrase—	The tides had rendered warm and balmy the coast. Rendered warm and balmy by the tides, the coast was ideal to bathe upon.
Present Participle Phrase —	In mankind the light is dawning.
	Dawning in mankind, the light shall enkindle man's heart.

We have in Chapter III learned how the thought which bears the modification in a sentence i.e. the Adjective or Adverb, can have a threefold expression: can move from word to phrase to clause:

into Noun with Prepositional Phrase	… he knoweth the shortness of his time.
	When the "Big Top" appeared on the outskirts of town was the moment most exciting in the year.
into Noun with Prepositional Phrase	The appearance of the "Big Top" on the outskirts of town was the most exciting moment in the year.
into Gerund	The most exciting of moments in the year was the Big Top ap- pearing on the outskirts of town.
	The pearl diver took a mammoth breath so that he would be able to stay ten minutes under water.
into Infinitive Phrase	The pearl diver took a mammoth breath (in order) to be able to stay ten minutes under water.
	The pearl diver took a mammoth breath to stay ten minutes under water.

Now as we move from sentences into clauses and clauses into phrases or direct from sentence to phrase and from phrases again into single words, "submerging," so we can move from words to phrases and then into clauses or into sentences: a creative falling to the elements and recombining into a harmonious whole, a consuming into ashes and rising again therefrom as the Phoenix bird, a fire process, this, within the creative fantasy, the conscious movement of the Word-Will. From the crystalline quality of the Simple Sentence, we move into the rhythmic binding flow of the Compound Sentence, to the wondrous point and counterpart, inward-outward, light and dark crescendo of the Complex Sentence, into the recreating, interweaving, conscious-formed Submerged Sentence. The threefold linguistic sheath man is given and born into as a speaking soul is the Sentences Simple, Compound, Complex. These, the only three types of sentence in language, remind us in their working and movement of the elements earth, water, and air or the atmosphere. But the fire element is added by man himself. He sparks the sheath and enkindles the tongue (language) by the conscious will of his own creative fantasy.

Simple Sentence —	Earth	given by
Compound Sentence —	Water	Nature
Complex Sentence —	Air	
Submerged (self-formed) Sentence	Fire	Created by the Human Self

The Creative Movement itself must be discovered in language, that man may learn to "move creatively."

Nature, human nature, and social custom or culture give him the language as he grows up into it. To own it as a Self, he must remove himself from the conscious interpenetration of it with his thought and will, and recreate its movements in his heart. The Sentence is the dynamic

the spires of the great shining towers…Up and down the great street as far as the eye could reach, the crowd was surging in the slow yet sinuous convolutions of an enormous brilliantly colored reptile. It seemed <u>to slide, to move, to pause, to surge, to writhe here and to be motionless</u> there in a gigantic and undulous rhythm that was infinitely complex and bewildering."

Prepositional Phrase

Out of the works of Charles Dickens:

"A blush <u>on the countenance of Monsieur,</u> the Marquis was no impeachment <u>of his high breeding</u>, it was not <u>from within</u>; it was occasioned <u>by an external circumstance</u>, beyond his control—the setting sun."

"Mr. Stryver had left them <u>in the passages</u>, to shoulder his way <u>back to the robing-room</u>. Another person, who had not joined the group, or interchanged a word <u>with any one of them</u>, but who had been leaning <u>against the wall</u> where its shadow was darkest, had silently strolled away. He now stepped <u>up to where Mr. Lorry and Mr. Darnay</u> stood <u>upon the pavement</u>."

"Here a long passage—what an enormous perspective I make <u>of it</u>!—leading <u>from Peggotty's kitchen</u>, <u>to the front door</u>. A dark storeroom opens <u>out of it</u>. and that is a place to be run past <u>at night</u>; for I don't know what may be <u>among those tubs and jars and old tea-chests</u>, when there is nobody <u>in there</u>, <u>with a dimly-burning light</u>, letting a moldy air come out <u>at the door</u>, in which there is a smell <u>of soap, pickles, pepper, candles, and coffee</u>, all <u>at one whiff</u>."

"Old Marley was as dead <u>as a door-nail</u>."

From Emerson's *History*:

"Genius detects <u>through the fly, through the caterpillar, through the grub, through the egg</u>, the constant individual; <u>through countless individuals</u>, the fixed species; <u>through many species</u>, the genus; <u>through all genera</u>, the steadfast type; <u>through all the kingdoms of organized life</u>, the eternal unity."

From Abraham Lincoln's Second Inaugural Address, for infinitive and prepositional phrases:

"<u>With malice toward none; with charity for all; with firmness in the right</u> as God gives us to see the right, let us strive on <u>to finish the work</u>, we are in; <u>to bind up the nation's wounds</u>; <u>to care for him</u>, who shall have borne the battle, and <u>for his widow</u>, and his orphan—to do all which may achieve and cherish a just and lasting peace <u>among ourselves</u> and <u>with all nations</u>."

Present Participle Phrase

"Singleton stepped in, advanced two paces, and stood <u>swaying slightly</u>. The sea hissed, flowed <u>roaring past the bows</u>, and the forecastle trembled, full of deep murmurs; the lamp flared, <u>swinging like a pendulum</u>."

"I, habitant of the Alleghenies, <u>treating of him</u> as he is in himself in his own rights,
<u>Pressing the pulse of the life that has seldom exhibited</u> itself, (the great pride of man in
        himself),
Chanter of Personality,<u> outlining what is yet to be,</u>
I project the history of the future."

"There, my voice announcing—I will sleep no more but arise. You oceans that have been
calm within me! How I feel you, fathomless, stirring, <u>preparing unprecedented waves and</u>
<u>storms</u>."

"And thou America,
Thy offspring <u>towering e'er so high</u>, yet higher Thee <u>above all towering</u>. With Victory on
thy left, and at they right hand Law;
Thou Union <u>holding all fusing, absorbing, tolerating all</u>
Thee, ever thee, I sing."

"Finally shall come the poet worthy that name,
The true son of God shall come <u>singing his songs</u>."
        —Walt Whitman, *Leaves of Grass*

"<u>Glancing down at his feet</u>, Captain Delano saw the freed hand of the servant <u>aiming with</u>
<u>a second dagger</u>—a small one, before concealed in his wool—with this he was snakishly
writhing up from the boats bottom, at the heart of his master, his countenance lividly vin-
dictive, <u>expressing the centered purpose of his soul</u>: while the Spaniard, half-choked, was
vainly shrinking away, with husky words incoherent to all but the Portuguese.

That moment, across the long-benighted mind of Captain Delano, a flash of revelation
swept, <u>illuminating in unanticipated clearness his host's whole mysterious demeanor</u>, with
every enigmatic event of the day, as well as the entire past voyage of the San Dominick."
        —Herman Melville, *Benito Cereno*

"All the world's a stage,
And all the men and women merely players:
They have their exits and their entrances;
And one man in his time plays many parts,
His acts <u>being seven ages</u>. At first the infant,
<u>Mewling and puking in the nurse's arms</u>.
And then the whining school-boy, with his satchel
And shining morning face, <u>creeping like snail</u>
<u>Unwillingly to school</u>. And then the lover,
<u>Sighing like furnace</u>, with a woeful ballad
Made to his mistress eyebrow. Then a soldier,
Full of strange oaths, and bearded like a pard,

"Let us go forth <u>refresh'd amid the day</u>.
Cheerfully tallying life, walking the world, the real,
<u>Nourish'd henceforth by our celestial dream</u>."
—Walt Whitman

"Love is both Creator's and Saviour's gospel to mankind, a volume <u>bound in rose— leaves,</u> <u>clasped with violets</u>, and, by the beaks of humming—birds, <u>printed with peach juice on</u> <u>the leaves of lilies</u>."
—Herman Melville

"When I perceive that men as plants increase,
<u>Cheered and check'd even by the self-same sky</u>…"
—Shakespeare, Sonnet XV

"<u>Seen at a little distance</u> as she walked across the churchyard and down the village, she seemed to be attired in pure white and her hair looked like the dash of gold on a lily."
—George Eliot, *Silas Marner*

"Thus situated, <u>employed in the most detestable occupation, immersed in a solitude</u>, where nothing could for an instant call my attention from the actual scene in which I was engaged, my spirits became unequal."
—Mary Shelly, Frankenstein

RELATIVE CLAUSE

From of the works of Ralph Waldo Emerson:

"All <u>that you call the world,</u> is the shadow of that substance, <u>which you are</u>, the perpetual creation of the powers of thought, of those <u>that are dependent</u> and of those that are independent of your will."

"This is the ultimate fact <u>which we so quickly reach on this</u>, as on every topic, the resolution of all into the ever-blessed One. Self-Existence is the attribute of the Supreme Cause, and it constitutes the measure of good by the degree in which it enters into all lower forms."

"We infer the spirit of the nation in great measure from the language, which is a <u>sort of</u> <u>monument to which each forcible individual in a course of many hundred years has con-</u><u>tributed a stone</u>."

"The word 'gentleman,' <u>which, like the word 'Christian', must hereafter characterize the</u> <u>present and the few preceding centuries by the importance attached to it</u>, is a homage to personal and incommunicable properties… An element, <u>which unites all the most forcible</u> <u>persons of every country, is somewhat so precise that it is at once felt if an individual lacks</u> <u>the Masonic sign</u>,—cannot be any casual product, but must be an average result of the character and faculties universally found in men."

"Thus men of character are the conscience of the society <u>to which they belong</u>."

fire, and burning a corpse, and plunging into that blackness of darkness, seemed the material counterpart of her monomaniac commander's soul."

"Though amid all the smoking horror and diabolism of a sea-fight, sharks will be seen longingly gazing up to the ship's decks, like hungry dogs round a table where red meat is being carved, ready to bolt down every killed man that is tossed to them; and though, while the valiant butchers over the deck table are thus cannibally carving each others' live meat with carving knives all gilded and tasseled, the sharks, also, with their jewel-hilted mouths, are quarrelsomely carving away under the table at the dead meat; and though were you to turn the whole affair upside down, it would still be pretty much the same thing, that is to say, a shocking sharkish business enough for all parties; and though sharks are the invariable outriders of all slave ships crossing the Atlantic, systematically trotting alongside, to be handy in case a parcel is to be carried anywhere, or a dead slave to be decently buried; and though one or two other instances might be set down, touching the set terms, paces, and occasions, when sharks do most socially congregate, and most hilariously feast; yet is there no conceivable time or occasion when you will find them in such countless numbers, and in gayer or more jovial spirits, than around a dead sperm whale, moored by night to a whale-ship at sea."

"If hereafter any highly cultured, poetical nation shall lure back to their birth-right, the merry May-day Gods of old; and lovingly enthrone them again in the now egotistical sky; in the now unhaunted hill; then be sure, exalted to Jove's high seat, the great Sperm Whale shall lord it."

"All sail being set, he now cast loose the life line, reserved for swaying him to the main royal-mast head! And in a few moments they were hoisting him thither, when, while but two thirds of the way aloft, and while peering ahead through the horizontal vacancy be tween the main-top-sail and top-gallant-sail, he raised a gull-like cry in the air, "there she blows!"—There she blows! A hump like a snow-hill! It is Moby Dick!"

"Be he Englishman, Frenchman, German, Dane or Scot; the European who scoffs at an American, calls his own brother "Raca," and stands in danger of the judgment. . . . We are not a nation, so much as a world; for unless we may claim all the world for our sire, like Melchisedec, we are without father or mother."

"There are certain ever-to-be-cherished moments in the life of almost any man, when a variety of little foregoing circumstances all unite to make him temporarily oblivious of whatever may be hard and bitter in his life, and also to make him most amiably and ruddily disposed; when the scene and company immediately before him are highly agreeable; and if at such a time he chance involuntarily to put himself into a scenically favorable bodily posture; then, in that posture, however transient, thou shalt catch the noble stature of his Better Angel; catch a heavenly glimpse of the latent heavenliness of man."

"We have lived before, and shall live again; and as we hope for a fairer world than this to come; so we came from one less fine. From each successive world, the demon Principle

law, and not the man, must have the credit of the conduct."
—William H. Prescott

"Go where he will, the wise man is at home."
—Ralph Waldo Emerson

Noun Clause

"I only regret <u>that I have but one life</u> to lose for my country."

—Nathan Hale, 1756–1776, said before his execution

"A teacher affects eternity; he can never tell <u>where his influence stops</u>."
—Henry Brook Adams

"<u>What I have done</u> will never perish."
—Napoleon

"This is the praise of Shakespeare <u>that his drama is the mirror of life</u>… Dryden pronounced <u>that Shakespeare was the man who, of all, modern and perhaps ancient, poets, had the largest and most comprehensive soul</u>."
—Samuel Johnson

"Earnest began to speak, giving to the people of <u>what was in his heart and mind</u>…Then all the people looked and saw <u>that what the deep—sighted poet said was true</u>…But Earnest, having finished <u>what he had to say</u>, took the poet's arm, and walked slowly homeward…"
—Nathaniel Hawthorne

"<u>Whoever has approved this idea of order, of the form of European, of English literature will not find it preposterous that the past should be altered by the present as much as the present is directed by the past</u>."
—T.S. Eliot

"If I should die think only this of me:
<u>That there's some corner of a foreign field</u>
<u>That is forever England</u>…"
—Rupert Brooke

"Out <u>where the skies are a trifle bluer</u>,
Out <u>where friendship's a little truer</u>.
That's <u>where the West begins</u>."
—Arthur Chapman

"<u>Whether the edifice now standing on the same site be the identical one to which she referred</u>, I am not antiquarian enough to know."
—Nathaniel Hawthorne

"Watch ye therefore: for ye know not when the master of the house cometh, at even, or at midnight, or at the cockcrowing, or in the morning: Lest coming suddenly he find you

Here, after beginning with a long Prepositional phrase, Poe introduces the Relative clause "which," and sets immediately into it the Subordinate "although," at whose end another Relative clause "who" have preceded them follows.

> "As when the summer comes from the south the snow-banks melt and the face of the earth becomes green before it, so shall the advancing spirit create its ornaments along its path, and carry with it the beauty it visits and the song which enchants it; it shall draw beautiful faces, warm hearts, wise discourse, and heroic acts, around its way, until evil is no more seen."
>
> —Ralph Waldo Emerson

Here we begin with a Subordinate clause "As...the snow-banks melt," which has immediately in it another Subordinate clause, like a bud in a flower, "when the summer comes from the south." Then, once in the main clause beginning "so shall the advancing spirit create," we have the Relative clause "it visits" modifying "beauty," and "which enchants it" modifying "song." We then move into another simple sentence, which renders the whole structure a Compound Sentence, beginning "it shall draw" after the semi-colon which serves for "and," and end with the Subordinate clause "until evil is no more seen," modifying the verb "draw."

> The Body of
> B. Franklin Printer.
> (Like the Cover of an old Book
> Its Contents torn out
> And stript of its Lettering & Gilding)
> Lies here, Food for worms.
> But the Work shall not be lost;
> For it will (as he believ'd) appear once more,
> In a new and more elegant Edition
> Revised and Corrected
> By the Author
>
> Benjamin Franklin's Epitaph,
> Written by Himself in 1728 at the Age of 22

Here we have a Compound Sentence in the second half of which is a double Subordinate clause. It reads, simplified:

> The Body of B. Franklin lies here, but the Work shall not be lost, for it will (as he believ'd) appear once more.

All other elements, the charm of the sentence, are phrases and appositions.

> she for thinking so), from that large shade—spreading, tall towering, deeply rooting, great tree took!

is just as possible and in proper places far more colorful than:

> Eve in her whimsy, say, or fantasy, perhaps, or even misapprehension, for she might have thought it by its color a pear (less keen she for thinking so) took an apple, golden t'was in hue (you thought "red") from that large shade-spreading, tall towering, deeply rooting (great) tree.

Of course the everyday order of prose in daily talk and most prosaic intellectual communication is in the S. V. O . form, even unto death! But the English, just to avoid this hurtling straight-laced legality of movement from the sovereign subject through proclamation (predication from Latin *"predicare"* means to proclaim) to his devoted subservient objects, invents and introduces the use of Phrase, especially the Participial Phrase, and more especially the Present Participial Phrase. Consider the simple text:

> A bee stung him.

Here we are laced in the S. V. O. order, unless we use the passive:

> He was stung by a bee.

which is less dynamic, more descriptive, thoughtful, like the distinction between the iambic and trochaic meters. How do we deal with the active form? Let us paint the picture, enact the scene, unfold the tune:

> "Where was he? — in the garden.

> What was he doing? — working: planting or trimming or weeding or the like.

We already have the start

> He was working in the garden.

Which we "distill" into its participial phrase:

> "working in the garden"

adding, perhaps, that preposition which strengthens this idea—"while." So, while working in the garden (Prepositional Participial) becomes our first phrase. Then we ask about the action itself, the verb "to sting." Did the bee just appear out of nowhere to complete the action, or did it "appear," did it enter the scene as it were? Certainly, at least it:

> flew over

to the man, perhaps even:

> from the cherry tree (prepositional).

So far, then, we've got:

> While working in the garden a bee flew over from the cherry tree and stung him.

thing, process or act. Only when they are found, is the human spirit satisfied. Their ordering is life itself, and what it is about. They can be consciously gathered and constructed into Sentence. Only through this Sixfold perspective is an event truly seen. Perceive them again:

> Before he met the giant who was ranging on the nearby river bank, the young shepherd bent down to pick up a stone, and after placing it carefully in his sling and twirling the sling with the utmost speed and grace, let fly the stone at the monster's brawny head, which, guided by the hand of God for the people's salvation, it hit, square in the middle, slaying him at once.

The seventh element, coming from the other side, as it were, is the reason or cause of the whole as such. Here we have included it prepositionally after God. In the previous example it remains latent or unexpressed.

Generally speaking a relative clause follows directly upon the noun it modifies, and the relative pronoun refers to the noun directly preceding it, though this rule is by no means unexceptional. Here this rule prevails, but the past participle phrase "guided by the hand of God…" coming as it does right behind "which," though it modify the "it" it preceded, can be ambiguously interpreted or heard as modifying the giant's brawny head. Now, philosophically, we might state a case for God's hand guiding the giant's head as well as the shepherd's stone, but grammatically, this interpretation is somewhat embarrassing. However, if read well, this sense need not be heard, though the use is not usual, but just so, stimulating, creating a more powerful effect. More conventionally the part in question would read:

> …let it fly at the monster's brawny head, which the stone, guided by the hand of God to save the people, hit square in the middle, slaying him at once.

Now let us work with this example rhetorically. We can first melt the beginning clauses to phrases:

> Meeting the giant ranging on the nearby river bank, the young shepherd, bending down to pick up a stone, placed it carefully in his sling, and twirling the sling with the utmost speed and grace, let fly the stone upon the monster, whose brawny head it hit—by God's hand guided—straight in the middle, slaying him at once to the people's salvation.

We have put the monster's head also in a Relative Clause, (which is as good a place as any for a monster's head). Thus the stone, aimed at the monster, hits his head, the action is taken up indirectly by the object. The emphasis above is put, this time on the placing of the stone in the sling, not the bending down to pick it up, which is put into participial phrase. Of course, all of the shepherd's actions could be put as participial phrase except the letting fly of the stone which is the "concentrate" of the whole verb movement. Again it could all be put in regular verb form as follows:

> Before he met the giant, ranging on the nearby river bank, the young shepherd bent down to pick up a stone, and after he had placed it in his sling, and twirled the sling with the utmost speed and grace, he let it fly, and guided by the hand of God for the people's salvation, the stone hit the monster's brawny head square in the middle and slew him at once.

Here apropos the style of the explanatory verb action assumes the Gerund, that is, becomes a noun. And God, of course, the explanation being "scientific," is dropped form the scene.

The effect of the action is the slaying. From this end we can affect the whole scene, putting it in the passive, and the preparatory action in the past perfect:

> Slain was the monster for the people's salvation by the hand of God guiding the stone the young shepherd, ere meeting him ranging near the river bank, had picked up, placed in his sling, twirled, with speed and grace, and let fly at the giant's brawny head, hitting him there square in the middle.

Having a double verb action, hit and slay, we can frame the whole scene in this action passively predicated:

> The monster was hit in the middle of his brawny head by the young shepherd's stone-guided by the hand of God for the people's salvation—which, ere meeting him ranging on the river bank, he had picked up, placed in his sling, twirled keenly, and let fly—and the giant was slain.

This rendition makes us aware by contrast of what the active voice in its most straightforward form would be:

> The shepherd slew the monster by flinging at him a stone picked up, placed, and twirled in his sling when they met at the river bank where the giant had been ranging, and through the guidance of the hand of God for salvation, hitting him with it in the center of his brawny forehead.

These are merely indications of rhetorical interplay of sentence elements, seaman's knots tied with the rope of Rhetoric, to serve as working models and act as stimulus to the fantasy and imagination. They should be analyzed, "undone" to study the loops therein, then varied further, changed, subtracted from and added to, worked over like clay or the tones of a musical key. Herewith the elements of the sentence can be grasped "in action" and one can practice using them.

We have been dealing rhetorically with those elements, which, when separated and put into individual sentences, would tell the story thus:

Activity of the Object:	Ranging on the nearby river bank was the giant
Subject:	The shepherd was young
Prior Activity of the Subject:	He bent down to pick up a stone, and placing it carefully in his sling, twirled the sling with the utmost speed and grace.
Action of the Subject:	Then they met and he let fly at him the stone
Object:	Brawny was the monster's head
Effect upon the Object:	It hit it right in the middle and slew him at once

language, latent or actual. By and by, this comes to expression, for it is the mark of what is unique in every individual. To the general speech he is bound by nature and culture. In the development of his own "style" man attains freedom.

The English Sentence is versatile and elastic, its movements manifold. It is pliable in ordering its elements, imaginative in arranging the furniture on its staging space, and colorful in its expression. Bountifully rich are the proclamations (predications) of its actors, generously given its scenery, and background. It is skillful in the technique of staging and choreography, and the musical accompaniment of its sounds and euphony dwell long upon the ear, delighting in the heart and soul.

POSITIONING OF PHRASES AND CLAUSES

(Phrases)

Typical positions of the participial phrases are directly before the subject and directly after it:

> Loaded down with all sorts of gifts stuffed in a huge sack, Santa Claus came down the chimney.

> The caravan arrived loaded with the spices, silks, and precious stones of the Orient.

> Sending its dawning light in advance to chase the night shadows and scatter the airy mists, the sun came rolling up over the horizon.

> They watched the sun setting in the West.

The "appositive position" of the participial phrase is also quite appropriate:

> John L. Sullivan, slugged silly by "Gentleman Jim," dropped the "himself" from his name after that famous fight.

> The rain, falling gently, pattered musically upon the window pane.

Phrases of time (adverbial) love the sentence beginning:

> At daybreak he rose, bathed, dressed, and set forth on his way.

> Before long the mule train appeared coming up out of the canyon.

and phrases of place and adverbs of manner usually follow suit:

> On a warm day long ago, in the flags by the river's edge all nestled in an ark of bulrushes, the Pharaoh's daughter found a weeping babe.

Again, such conventions of ordering of phrases and clauses are not overly rigid:

> Bold with his sense of mission
> and spirited with charge, at the
> sound of the clock striking one, middle
> of the night, Paul Revere, from the
> opposite shore, set forth on his famous ride.

Prepositional Phrases can be anywhere and everywhere (at once), as before shown, and the

To practice the positioning of Phrases let us build up a series round the simple sentence:

The eagle flies.

A host of Phrases occur immediately. With them we can paint the scene. Start with the Prepositional "down from the crag":

The eagle flies down from the crag.

He is "in search for prey" or "eager for prey":

The eagle flies down from the crag in search for prey.

He is a "bold and keen-eyed" hunter. So:

The eagle flies down from the crag in search for prey, bold and keen-eyed.

Here a keen grammarian might say: Bold and keen-eyed is an adjective proper consisting of two words; hence it should have a position directly upon the noun it modifies. This is not necessarily so: but, we shall give it an "appositive position" anyway:

The eagle, bold and keen-eyed, flies down from the crag in search of prey.

How does he fly? "Swift as the wind." Let us think where the phrase might best fit. Expressing the quality of the verb action, perhaps it should follow the verb:

The eagle, bold and keen-eyed, flies swift as the wind down from the crag in search of prey.

Or should the almost idiomatic connection of "flies" with "down from the crag," which also sounds good, retain that position, and the qualitative adverb follow? Thus:

The eagle, bold and keen-eyed, flies down from the crag swift as the wind in search of prey.

We might add the time "in the early morning hours"

The eagle, bold and keen-eyed, flies down from the crag swift as the wind in search of prey in the early morning hours.

This is a travelogue. So far we have five modifying phrases all hung up after the subject, four of them following the verb, in no especially happy order. Even this lop-sided predication could perhaps be improved by putting "in the early morning hours" elsewhere, but obviously the main improvement is to begin using the left side of the sentence (before the subject).

In the early morning hours, the eagle, bold and keen-eyed, flies down from his mountain crag in search of prey and swift as the wind.

Swift as the wind in the early morning hours, the eagle, bold and keen-eyed, flies down from the crag in search of prey.

In search of prey in the early morning hours the bold and keen-eyed eagle, swift as the wind flies down from his mountain crag.

These are attempts. It is a question of sound and rhythm and ease of pronunciation (euphony) as well as meaning. There are only so many combinations of the elements. Theoretically they could and actually should be tried, till one or two favorable arrangements are found. Let's try a few more:

a picture "over or across the plain," and increase the eagle's image "soaring on mighty wing" and then for depth in contrast add another source of action (some subject acting in subordination), as e.g. "as the ground hogs begin peeping out of their holes," "or after the coyote has turned in from his nightly prowls," etc.

> From his crag on the mountain in the early morn, just after the coyote has turned in from his nightly prowls, the eagle, bold and keen-eyed and swift as the wind, flies down across the plain soaring on mighty wings in search of prey.

> In the early morning hour when the ground hog begins to peep out of its hole the bold and keen-eyed eagle flies soaring on mighty wing down from the mountain crag out over the plain as swift as the wind in search of prey.

To this text, the silver inlay of the "minor" may, if desired, be worked in.

Again, we give but indications here. A "style" must be practiced. The most prosaic business letter, the most profound theological text have the same elements and require identical treatment. Only, with literary texts, where the pictorial element is greater and more vivid, this practice in rhetorical movement is easiest and most enjoyable. What it exercises, above all, is consciousness of the elements and the alphabet of sentence movement, grammatically and rhetorically. Now take similar simple sentences: the ship sails, the pancho (or Indian) rides, the mountain climber (the "sherpa") climbs, the train passes, rolls, rides, the flowers bloom, the snow melts, the lion roars, the lawyer pleads his case, the surgeon operates, the pilot flies, the painter paints, the hunters chase (the fox), the fox runs, the fish (salmon, shark, seal) swims, etc., or yet others, and treat them the same, practicing with added clauses and phrases the techniques before delineated, the positioning here exhibited, and the "balancing" of the two regions—Phrase and Clause—within the Sentence.

We are herewith arrived at this book's close.

c) of emphasizing the middle (breast) region, where it can circulate in "Answer form" through the sentence attaching externally as adverb and adjective, or be drawn in inwardly to inner experience as Noun Clause proper, connecting the first two like the hypotenuse of a right triangle.

And, thus subordinating, the sentence creates the linguistic force lines that build into our consciousness the sense of the figure of language, with a macrocosmic dimension in the earth globe, and a microcosmic dimension in the human body: head, breast, limbs.

Then in this threefold clausal composition of the Sentence the fourfold form of Phrase is seen as it rises up out of the Clause's subject-verb polarity and now appears free from this polar axis in dynamic weaving form. Yet these Phrases themselves, in their freed movement, condense on the one hand into the Infinitive Phrase containing the verb power in its unrealized or "ideal" state, spoken of as yet unraveled into time and space, and, on the other hand diffuse into the explicating concretizing Prepositional Phrase, giving position and direction; carrying the verb action and placing the noun content everywhere and every way into the Real, or Temporal-Spatial, in fine, into the world. Thus in the weaving axis-free being of the phrase do the two poles form themselves anew. And the Participial Phrases build the bridge between these two by transforming the predicated verb action of the subject into the subject's own attribute, so that the doing and experiencing of the subject in life and the world expressed in the verb becomes the character and property of the subject as the Past Participial Phrase, and as the Present Participial Phrase is the activity and attribute flowing from the subject, surrounding it as atmosphere and environment characterizing its present state.

So after the Sentence orders itself as a whole into a structure, showing this structure as a *prime movement*, then out of the infinity of words, in proportion to this polar structural movement, there condenses into view the force field of the Clause, showing itself in a prime form, in which the Polarity of Structure (Subject: Apposition—Verb: Object) specifies to a foundational "axis"(subject-verb). And from this axial force field of the Clause a second higher sphere, that of the Phrase can free itself, be born, and form, mirroring in its fourness, as just shown, the dynamic axis-turn of the Clause. Now this is a living, creative process manifest static in what is at first sight seen when the ordinary Sentence of ordinary language is studied from the perspective of what here is called its Structure and its Composition.

III   We continued to the parts of speech, the organs of a Sentence, as modes of enterprise and activity: naming, acting, attributing, adverbing, prepositioning, conjoining, exclaiming, pre-naming, and saw into a yet higher sphere of Sentence meaning, where a transcending movement in the inner state of consciousness itself is reflected in the experience of the "octave" movement from Pronoun duality to the Noun-Verb-Duality. Through the pronoun the language first becomes inner human speech, for the "I" is first given as pronoun or pre-name. Here we discern a *prime consciousness*, and the scale of awakening moves from this lower pre-naming state to the awareness "I and the World," on whose octave level the above "organ" activities can be called into play.

At last we see the Sentence move in its own right—the self-unfolding, self-forming activity of the Sentence in its creative "submerging-emerging" consciousness—wherein it redeems, as

V a quintessence, the virtues of the Complex-Compound-Simple Sentences given by Nature (for we grow up speaking) and Culture (for one learns the modes of the day). Here is Man in his task as self-creative agent in the sphere where he is first and truly a Self, namely, *in Speaking*—where the word is flowing o'er the tongue: Language; or where the flow is held in a form: Grammar.

And here the same polarity skeletally visible in structure, then in the ascending movement of composition, in the inner octave of the organs, in the balance of Soul Mood between the subjunctive spirit heights and the imperative earthly depths, has become in metamorphosis the life essential movement of the human Self as such, namely, the conscious penetrating of the threefold Sentence—corporeality, the mastering of the elements that round the Nature and Culture given language, and, with the fire of the creative spirit transforming these, transmitting the already made into a making—into the making of a self-created style. This is the *prime self-movement* of man.

At the close through the rounded arch of rhetoric we find again the foundational polarity, met at the start, but now, all comprehending, in the Seven Great Rhetorical Elements—the Six and

VI the One—out of which all language and all learning of our human intelligence originates. We behold language in the grand arc of its full movement and meaning: the prior activity of the Subject, the subject, the action of the Subject, the activity of the Object, the Object, the effect with or upon the Object—this sixfold manifestation of creative being met from the other side by the cause or leader of its movement, which renders it into reason, as does the moon (and the man therein!) meet the light of the all-encompassing Sun, who has sent its being in the powers of its six prime colors into the earth and earth aura, leading it there into the cool rays of the star-bounded reflection.

So with the prime movement of Sentence Structure, the prime form of Sentence composition, the prime consciousness of Sentence Organs, the prime mood of Sentence Mood, the prime self-movement of Sentence Movement, and the prime colors and prime cause of Sentence order, we traverse the realm of the Word "from end to end with labor keen," perceive its name in the perspective of a true consciousness, and create the organ of clarity we need to allow us to move with the will of the word in true speech.